à Kempis Thomas

The Little Garden of Roses and Valley of Lilies

Now first correctly translated from the original Latin

à Kempis Thomas

The Little Garden of Roses and Valley of Lilies
Now first correctly translated from the original Latin

ISBN/EAN: 9783337082758

Printed in Europe, USA, Canada, Australia, Japan

Cover: Foto ©Lupo / pixelio.de

More available books at **www.hansebooks.com**

TO THE

Rev. JOHN McCLOSKEY, &c.

PASTOR OF ST. JOSEPH'S CHURCH, NEW YORK,

Whose unaffected piety as a Christian Divine, splendid talents as an effective Preacher, extensive acquirements as an elegant Scholar, and dignified yet amiable manners as an accomplished Gentleman, have long been the admiration, the ornament, and the model of his devoted flock,

THIS LITTLE WORK IS RESPECTFULLY DEDICATED

BY HIS

FORMER PARISHIONERS,

AND

Much obliged humble servants,

THE PUBLISHERS.

NEW YORK,
    Eve of the Feast of the Nativity.

PREFACE.

In the midst of the alarming indifference and deplorable incredulity of the age, we ought to regard as peculiarly predestinated to happiness eternal, all those who, despite of every allurement, every seduction, and every temptation to error held out by a vain world,—have continued inviolably attached to the one true Faith :—the source of all virtues, and the only foundation of moral as well as of religious perfection. They at least know the nature of man's origin,—why he has been placed for some time a sojourner on this earth,—what he ought to do while here,—and what he is destined to become hereafter, at the termination of a transient career. The rule of life adopted by these pious souls, is not swayed by chance, caprice, blind instinct, or the cravings of mere animal existence. While anxious to extend, enlighten, and exalt the powers of the understanding, faith is ever kept in view, as the regulator and director of the heart ;—purifying all its affections, and diffusing throughout a delicious peace: thus while ever watchfully and indefatigably employed in clearing away the obstructions in the road towards the joys of heaven, it already constitutes happiness on earth.

But to recognize all the beauties of virtue, to taste all the sweets of piety, and present to the eyes of erring man, a true and *efficient* model of a Christian Life, we must not rest strictly within the boundaries which separate faith from irreligion, and the dominion of morality from that of the vices and passions. This middle way—*via media*—hemmed in by so many reservations in favour of the gratification of the senses,—of pride, —of worldly interests,—ever dissatisfied, and too much taken up with mundane attachments,—is consequently cold and indifferent, sullied with numerous defects, deprived of divine consolations, and always exposed to the most dangerous tendencies of falling into sin. It exhibits an incessant vaccillation between good and bad—between virtue and vice: like the feeble and languishing life of a man who confining himself to a portion of nourishment barely sufficient to keep him from the jaws of death, may

PREFACE. vii

struggle out a sickly existence, but he will undoubtedly fall under the first attack of a violent malady.

To prevent the grievous and inevitable consequences of a life led in this manner, — of an habitual tepidity, — of a sloth which is in direct opposition to the sublime precepts and elevated hopes of faith, it is absolutely necessary to enter with a generous courage on the road of christian practice. For this end we must above all things, be fully penetrated with the spirit of our Saviour, JESUS CHRIST, and apply ourselves to thoroughly understand His thoughts, His words, and His actions; in order to render our thoughts, words, and actions in all things conformable to His. For, *whatever* JESUS CHRIST *has done in the flesh for all men, that, every one of us is obliged to do for himself.* It is only in this way, we can participate in the fruits of the redemption, and merit the glorious title of children of GOD:—*If any man have not the spirit of* CHRIST, *he is none of His Whosoever are led by the spirit of* GOD, *they are the Sons of* GOD.* It is then indispensable to disengage our Christian sentiments from

* Rom. viii. 9, and 14.

the impure intermixture of worldly ideas—from secular prejudices by which they are obscured and corrupted if not entirely strangled. This is the first and paramount requisite of a life truly Christian.

We must not however confine our efforts to beautiful speculations, or brilliant theories,—to vain projects of ideal perfection,—to reading and meditation without profit. We must come to practice,—to practice full of serious earnestness,—to a daily and sustained application of Christian maxims, in all the circumstances of our thoughts, our projects, our enterprises, and our occupations. In all situations, in all the vicissitudes of life,—in prosperity and adversity, in health and in sickness,—all our thoughts, words, and actions ought to be inspired, regulated, and directed by the principles of our holy faith and of christian morality. If our soul is deeply penetrated with these principles and filled with these sentiments, they will be reproduced and realized without difficulty in all our connexions with mankind. From the spirit of humility and of charity, with which our hearts shall be penetrated, will be diffused over our whole exterior, an amiable modesty, a mildness, a delightful amenity, which will enable all who approach us to perceive that God is in all our actions, and that we are actuated by His divine influence. There will exhale, as it were, from our whole person, an odour of sanctity, which will bring back the thoughts of God and of virtue into souls of the most abandoned character.

And although the faithful practice of these evangelical virtues may cost us not a little, shall we not be most amply recompensed for all our trouble by the immediate result of these virtues?

How many are the evils from which they will deliver us? In what numberless ways can they not alleviate the burden of these evils interwoven with our earthly sojourn? What joy and serenity will they not maintain in our souls? What undiminished confidence, what mutual condescension, what heavenly peace, will they not diffuse in every domestic circle? And although the world forsakes us, and although doomed to experience desolation within and without, can there be anything painful, anything terrible, to a christian, who has his mind and thoughts fixed on heaven? What can he fear, and for what may he not hope,—he who has for his defense and support, the arm of the MOST HIGH?

Among the productions, which are powerfully adapted to nourish and sustain the fervour of pious souls, and kindle it anew in lukewarm christians, must be placed in the first rank, the works of these pious monks and hermits, who after quitting the world, its vain pleasures, and idle illusions, passed their lives in subduing their passions,—in probing and purifying the most secret folds of their hearts,—in contemplating the things of heaven, and in advancing every day still farther in the way of perfection. Such among others are the works of *Thomas à Kempis* in the 15th, and of *Louis le Blois* in the following century. Their works form a real treasure of piety, and it has been long a cause of regret, that they have not been better known and more generally circulated.

The principal works of piety written by *Thomas à Kempis*, (exclusive of the *Imitation of Christ*, which some deny to be his,) are the *Little Garden of Roses*, and the *Valley of Lilies*. These two (of which a *correct* translation is now for the first time presented to the pious reader,) possess advantages over the *Imitation* itself;—inasmuch as they are more practical, more in detail, better adapted to the individual wants of the faithful, and more within the comprehension of the many. Persons of every rank and condition, will here find an inexhaustible fund of the most solid advice, of the sagest counsels, and of the various maxims applicable to their particular state, interior and exterior.

The instructions of *Thomas à Kempis* are addressed to religious communities, who were not entirely shut out from the world by the impassable barrier of the cloister. They were consequently exposed to the contagion of its maxims and examples. It is against these dangers, that the pious author wishes to protect them. Dangers similar to these, and even still greater, await christians who live altogether in the world, and who have not the advantage of refreshing and renewing their pious dispositions, every day in the solitude and holy exercises of a religious house. The *Little Garden of Roses* and *Valley of Lilies* are therefore perfectly adapted to their spiritual wants.

There can be no doubt, that these two little works will contribute largely to the moral and religious amelioration of those who will read them with *suitable dispositions*: for that which causes many christians to lose much of the good fruit, which they might otherwise derive from spiritual reading, is, the careless, inefficient manner in which it is performed. Those who wish to read with profit, are earnestly requested to leisurely peruse the following instructions; which are a compendium of all that have been handed down on this subject, by the masters and directors of a spiritual life.—

RULES FOR PIOUS READING.

1. Before reading as before prayer, prepare thy soul to receive the outpouring of the divine grace. For this end determine on a certain time for reading, and during this time, forget the world and all the affairs thereof; keep thy soul steadily fixed on God, and look on Him only. Invoke His light, and His inspiration, and dispose thyself to follow them in every particular.

2. Apply all thy mind to the subject of thy reading. Read leisurely, atten-

tively, and without a spirit of curiosity or of criticism. Pause when GOD vouchsafes to speak to thy heart, and pass not on from one chapter, until thou wilt have extracted the favours and graces, which GOD has there enclosed for thy benefit.

3. Sum up with devout and tender affection, the pious thoughts, with which thou hast been entertained; form resolutions on each particular; and foresee the occasions which may be presented of putting in practice the instructions and information derived. Thank GOD for the graces, which He has vouchsafed to grant, and for the pious thoughts with which He has inspired thee. Implore the strength, necessary to accomplish what He requires at thy hands, and recal from time to time,—for instance,—at the striking of the clock, or the toll of the bell,—the promises made to thy CREATOR and SOVEREIGN LORD. At night, compare thy conduct, during the day, with the resolutions made in the morning; deplore in the presence of GOD, the sins with which thou canst charge thy conscience; humbly hope for the pardon promised the contrite and penitent heart; renew thy holy purpose

of being more faithful for the future;— beg the aid of the divine grace, and always recommence with fresh ardour and renewed courage. Be punctual and exact in following this simple and easy plan in all thy reading and meditation, and God will load thee with benefits and blessings in all abundance.

THE DEVOUT CHRISTIAN MAY REAP MUCH BENEFIT BY OBSERVING THE FOLLOWING METHOD

OF HOLY MEDITATION.

Be mindful of thy last end, and thou shalt never sin.*

All the earth is made desolate because there is none that thinketh in his heart.†

Reflections made on certain truths for the purpose of becoming better, is called *Meditation*.

To meditate then is to reflect,—to think seriously.

To be saved, it is necessary to meditate; because there can be no salvation,

* Eccli. vii. 40. † Jer. xii.

without reflection on the means of obtaining it.

We must meditate to be fully penetrated with the great truths of salvation, and to conform our life and manners to that object.

We must meditate to be enabled to fight with courage against the three great enemies of our salvation,—the devil, the world, and ourselves.

We must meditate for the purpose of attaining a knowledge of God and of ourselves.

We must meditate to conquer our passions, and to clearly comprehend the misfortune of those who may have abandoned themselves to their destructive sway.

We must meditate to fully conceive the vanity of all sublunary things, and to detach ourselves therefrom.

In fine we must meditate to obtain an Imitation of Jesus Christ, who is the model, after which we should copy; and according to which we shall be judged.

* We can meditate on all subjects connected with God, our salvation, the correction of our defects and the practice of virtue.

MANNER OF MEDITATING.

To meditate with profit, we must—

1. Place ourselves in the presence of God and adore Him.
2. Reflect on our sins, and make an act of contrition.
3. Unite ourselves to JESUS CHRIST; for without Him we can do nothing pleasing to God.
4. Implore the light of the HOLY GHOST; whereas without His aid we cannot form even one good thought.

☞ This is termed the *Preparation.*

We must afterwards —

1. Ponder on the subject or important truth, on which we desire to meditate: such as the *Certainty of Death*, the *Terrors of the Last Judgment*, the *Fear of Hell*, the *Joys of Heaven*, &c., &c.
2. Excite in the heart, holy sentiments and tender affections on that particular subject, or important truth.
3. After these reflections and pious sentiments, we must take an introspective view of ourselves, to examine first regarding the past, how we have conducted ourselves in reference to the subject under meditation; afterwards to examine how we are disposed for the pres-

ent; and lastly to form resolutions for the future. We must not however content ourselves with general resolutions, we must always form our resolutions, by particulars,—each one by itself; in order to put them afterwards in practice.

This is called the *Body or Substance of the Meditation*.

To conclude our Meditation, we must—

1. Thank God for having permitted us to appear in His presence, and for the grace, which He vouchsafed to grant, during our Meditation.

2. Ask pardon for our distractions.

3. Offer up our resolutions, and implore the grace of God to accomplish them.

4. Place our resolutions under the protection of the Blessed Virgin.

5. Finally, make choice of some holy thought, with which we have been particularly affected: or of some pious sentiment in connection with the subject of our meditation, in order to recall it to mind sometimes during the day: this is termed a Spiritual Nosegay.

ADVICE ON MEDITATION.

For a due consideration of the subject, every one should ask himself:—

1. What ought I believe and know on this subject?
2. What ought I do in reference to this subject?
3. What have I done up to the present time?
4. What shall I do for the future?
5. How and by what means shall I do it?

To produce suitable affections we should excite the following sentiments:

1. Sorrow for our sloth, our tepidity, and our numerous defects.
2. A firm resolution of correcting ourselves.
3. Watchful distrust of our fickleness and weakness.
4. To call forth sentiments of the love of God, and to excite ourselves to overcome all difficulties in the way of our eternal salvation.

In the name of our Lord Jesus Christ, the pious Reader is earnestly requested to pray for the spiritual welfare of

THE TRANSLATOR.

CONTENTS.

GARDEN OF ROSES.

CHAP.		PAGE.
1.	On seeking the company of the good, and flying that of the bad	1
2.	On flying the world, and the snares of the devil	5
3.	True wisdom must be sought of God	10
4.	On warring against our own vices	13
5.	On the necessity of acquiring the grace of devotion	18
6.	Of hearing and reading the divine word	20
7.	On divine consolation in tribulation	24
8.	On the joy of a good conscience in the Holy Spirit	28
9.	On the edifying demeanor of an humble brother	33
10.	On the instability of the human heart	40
11.	On trust in God in time of trouble	45
12.	On the efficacy of prayer, and the advantages of pious reading	49
13.	On the praises of charity and its fruits	61
14.	On watching and striving against temptations	70
15.	On bearing one another's burthens	73
16.	On the love of Christ, and hatred of the world	80
17.	On the imitation of the most holy life of our Lord Jesus Christ	90
18.	On the eternal praise of God	100

CONTENTS.

THE VALLEY OF LILIES.

CHAP.	PAGE.
Prologue	115
1. On the three-fold state of human life	117
2. On the praise of God, during the barrenness or tepidity of devotion	123
3. On the probation of the just by adversity	127
4. Of the true lover of God	130
5. On the gratitude of the soul, for every good	133
6. On the conformity of the devout soul to the cross	136
7. On the walking of a pure soul with God	138
8. On the peace of heart, and rest in God	141
9. On recollection of the heart with God	144
10. On watching and prayer against temptations	147
11. On the fear of eternal punishment, as a preservative against the vices of the flesh and pride of spirit	152
12. On the memory of our Lord's passion, as a remedy against dissipation or distraction of mind	156
13. On the invocation of the holy name of Jesus, and of the blessed Mary, His Virgin Mother	161
14. On the necessity of struggling manfully against vice, after the example of the saints	169
15. On the love of retirement and holy perseverance	174
16. On divine consolation in tribulation for Christ's sake	177
17. On watching over the conscience, in every place and at all times	182

CONTENTS.

18 On solitude and silence . . . 189
19 On the refuge of the poor, in God their helper 199
20. On the poor and sick Lazarus . . 205
21. On the clear understanding of the Holy Scriptures 211
22. On the great merit of patience for the sake of Christ 219
23. On the good conversation of the humble christian 222
24. On prudent conversation, and brotherly compassion 226
25. On the uncertain hour of death, and the speedy end of this life . . 232
26. On the eternal praise of God, and the desire of eternal glory . . . 241
27. Of the praises sung by the holy Angels in Heaven 249
28. A prayer of the devout lover of God . 253
29. On union of the heart with God . . 258
30. On true peace, to be sought for in God alone 264
31. That our intention should be pure and always directed towards God . 269
32. The prayer of an humble and a contrite spirit 275
33 Of holy fellowship with Jesus and with his saints 278
34 On placing our sovereign good and farthest aim in God alone . . 289

THE
Garden of Roses.

THE LITTLE GARDEN OF ROSES.

CHAP. I.

ON SEEKING THE COMPANY OF THE GOOD, AND FLYING THAT OF THE BAD.

"*Cum sancto sanctus eris, et cum perverso perverteris.*"*

"*With the holy, thou wilt be holy; and with the perverse, thou wilt be perverted.*"

1. Be diligently on thy guard, beloved brother in Christ, lest thou be seduced by the company of false and wicked men, or of those who

* Ps. xvii. 26.

live without discipline; but draw near to the virtuous, to those who are friends of order and to the well instructed; from whom thou wilt only hear words that are good, full of comfort and edification.

For as the unkindled coal warms and glows when thrown on a burning fire, so a lukewarm Christian, in the company of a pious and fervent brother, often recovers his piety and fervour; and as he grows in the knowledge of good, acquires also the sweet odour of virtue.

It was thus that the apostles, from following Christ, became holy men, and received the fulness of the Holy Spirit.

It was thus that Mark from following St. Peter, became learned in the holy gospel; which with much gladness he heard from the very lips of that blessed apostle.

It was thus that by following St.

Paul, Timothy became learned in the Holy Scriptures which he had studied from his early youth; and furthermore, when the grace of God advanced in him, was ordained bishop, at Ephesus, by the master who loved him, as a loving father does his only child.

2. It was thus that Polycarp, the disciple of Saint John the Apostle, became a glowing preacher of the faith to the people, and suffered with Saint Ignatius a glorious martyrdom;—that our blessed father Augustine, instructed and baptized by Saint Ambrose, became that glorious doctor of the holy Church, whose fame is spread over all the earth;—and so of that holy youth Maurus, who, following the footsteps of Saint Benedict, was thereafter, by God's blessing, a holy abbot, as famed for his virtues as for his miracles.

And thus it was that Bernard, that man well beloved of God, in the school of the venerable Stephen, Abbot of Citeaux, became the light of religion in his order: shining like a clear star in the firmament.

Innumerable are the examples, both ancient and modern, which prove that the society of the good tends to the safety of the soul, and that of the wicked to its perdition; that good instruction is profitable, and evil conversation dangerous; and that silence and solitude increase our spiritual advancement, while the dissipation and tumult of the world retard its growth.

Then either live alone as much as possible and labour in the service of God; or join thyself to the devout and holy, with whom thou mayest discourse on the virtues of Jesus Christ.

But see that thou dost not fathom through vain curiosity, the holy mysteries of religion ; seek rather to search into thy own faults, and to apply to the wounds of thy soul, all necessary and wholesome remedies.

CHAP. II.

ON FLYING THE WORLD, AND THE SNARES OF THE DEVIL.

" *Audiens, sapiens, sapientior erit.*"*

" *A wise man shall hear, and shall be wiser.*"

1. Young man, who yet lovest virtue, hearken to the words of eternal wisdom ; from these thou wilt

* Prov. i. 5.

draw more instruction than from the combined discourse of all the wisdom of the world.

According to the words of the Apostle St. John; "Love not the world, nor the things which are in the world."* Cast them away as dung—reject them as poison.

Think always of eternity, and temptations shall cease to allure.

Avoid every thing that may hurt thy soul: be not an object of scandal to any one: and watch well that thou drop not one unbecoming word.

Should thy father according to the flesh seek to turn thee from the service of God, answer him that thou hast a Father who is in heaven. Should thy mother or sister oppose the execution of thy designs, tell them they are mortal, and may be deceived; adding,

* 1 John ii. 15.

"He who made me, He shall guide me."

He that gives himself up to the service of God, shall want for nothing.

Commend to the keeping of God all thy friends; pray for their conversion and perseverance in welldoing; ask above all that their attachment to the things of this world may never make them offend God, and thereby lose the kingdom of heaven.

The dissipation of frequent visits will bring trouble on thy soul. The world passes away, and the concupiscence thereof.*

Even so thou also shalt pass away, and all that are dear to thee.

2. "Many are the snares of the devil, and they that are anxious to become rich, or great, fall into

---

* 1 John ii. 17.

temptation, and into many unprofitable and hurtful desires."*

We have daily snares in our meat and drink, in our wandering eye, our idle tongue, the inconstancy of our hearts, and distaste for good works.

Honour, riches, and power, are but vanity; and what seekest thou in the world, or what dost thou desire to see in the world, which is nothing and vanity? for all is vanity, frailty, and deceit, except the love of God, and perseverance in well-doing.

Thou canst not love God perfectly, till thou despisest thyself, and the world, for the love of God, who will render thee " an hundred fold now in this time, and in the world to come life everlasting."†

3. Oh, fellow pilgrim and brother, let it not seem hard to be with-

* 1 Tim. vi. 9. † Mark x. 30.

drawn from thy friends and acquaintance, who are often an obstacle to thy eternal salvation, and the means of lessening the divine consolations.

Where are those friends with whom thou hast laughed and sported? Alas! I know not:—they are gone, and I am left alone. Where are the visions of yesterday? They have melted away. Where is our meat and our drink? They are past for ever. And have thy privations been injurious, or hath thy abstinence been hurtful?—Thou must reply that they have hurt thee not at all. Therefore is not he alone wise who renounces the world and its pleasures for the service,—the reasonable service,—of God? Most assuredly he is. Woe to all those whom the world inebriates with its charms; for soon all pleasant company flieth away, and is lost in death. Behold! all those I loved are dead, and never more will they return : nay I too shall soon follow them at the call of God. They were as passing guests on earth— I too am a pilgrim. They have left all—as I must forsake all. As a shadow they have passed away —I too like them shall pass away.

CHAP. III.

TRUE WISDOM MUST BE SOUGHT OF GOD.

"*Beatus vir, qui invenit sapientiam.*"*

"*Blessed is the man that findeth wisdom.*"

1. Seek the true wisdom, which

* Prov. iii. 13.

Christ hath taught us, and pointed out by his example.

He is truly wise who hates iniquity, who speaks the truth, and works the works of justice:—who leads a sober and chaste life, who is pious, humble, and devout; and who shuns the perilous rocks of temptation:—he possesses true wisdom, and is pleasing to God. He enjoys the favour of men—his conscience is pure—sorrow assails him not—peace is his possession—and God often pours into his breast, consolations, that the world can neither know nor relish.

2. But the wisdom of the world is vanity, and is reputed as foolishness in the sight of God. It leads into error those that love it, and finally becomes their torment. For the wisdom of the flesh is the death of the soul, and striketh alike both those who give themselves up to

the alluring pleasures of sense and those who wallow in delights; for pain and sorrowful regret are all that remain after the shameful enjoyments of the flesh.

But true wisdom is drawn from the profound words and holy actions of Christ; by which He invites us to despise the world, to fly from its pleasures, to curb our flesh, to bear with sorrow, to bow to toil, and to cherish virtue.

CHAP. IV.

ON WARRING AGAINST OUR OWN VICES.

"*Regnum cœlorum vim patitur.*"*

"*The kingdom of heaven suffereth violence.*"

1. Many begin well, yet few persevere; but how very small is the number of those who attain perfection!

For either we too easily fall before the allurements of the flesh, or we are puffed up with pride, or we are cast down by adversity.

Alas! how seldom is found one who loves God purely, overcomes himself completely, and makes an entire renunciation of all his affections.

* Matt. xi. 12.

"Perfection," said a devout person, "is a rare bird; because it is too difficult to overcome oneself." But he that works not hard to attain virtue, shall never be filled with its sweetness.

Every virtue hath a sweetness peculiar to itself, to refresh him that worketh well; but he that clings to vice, begets for himself an evil end, makes shipwreck of his honour, destroys repose, lays up a store of infirmities, increases sorrow, and deprives himself of the relish of what is good and virtuous. But he that denies himself lawful pleasures, increases the surety of resisting such as are unlawful.

2. He that muzzles the mouth of the hound, needs not fear his bark; so he that keeps strict silence shall not offend with his lips.

He that willingly lives retired and in silence, is far removed from falsehood and bickering;—from evil speaking and detraction;—from anger and murmuring.

He that hearkens not to evil discourses, and shuts his eyes on the vanities of this world, more easily avoids its snares, and turns away his thoughts from its vain imaginations: for a watch over the senses is the foundation of purity, the discipline of peace, and the mirror of devotion.

When wrath takes possession of the breast, wisdom takes to flight even from the wise. He that speaks hastily is like a snarling hound; but a meek answer breaks the violence of wrath, and gives to the afflicted, roses in the stead of thorns.

Blessed is the prudent tongue; for it heals the wounds of the angry.

3. He that resisteth his evil inclinations in their birth, and whilst

they are yet weak, shall more easily destroy them than when they will have acquired more strength.

4. He that is constant in the heavenly exercises of prayer and meditation, is like the prudent gardener, who plants roses and lilies in his borders—and has sweet joy in store: for he will greatly rejoice hereafter with the holy angels, in the heavenly paradise.

He that preserves purity in soul and body is like the holy angels; but he that yields to his evil inclinations, and takes pleasure in the depravity of his thoughts, is the bondslave of Satan.

It may be a hard struggle to resist the seductions of vice; but it shall be a much harder punishment to awake in the fire of hell, there to be tormented forever.

One heat allays another; and nail drives out nail; but idle laughter is put to flight by a grave and edifying sadness.

When the love of God enters the heart, all earthly and transitory affections flee away.

He is wise that can despise the countless allurements of this world. The dignities of the tiara or the crown, with all their privileges, are as nothing: the end of all is death and the grave, worms, and ashes. How high soever man may exalt himself, he is nothing—death strips him of all Happy is that pilgrim whose home is in heaven.

CHAP. V.

ON THE NECESSITY OF ACQUIRING THE GRACE OF DEVOTION.

"*Væ vobis, qui ridetis, quia flebitis.*"*

"Woe to you that laugh, for you shall weep."

1. As virtue cannot exist with vice, so devotion is not to be acquired in the joyousness of feast and festival, but in sorrow and silence.

Perfection in virtue cannot be obtained at once, but by little and little;—by much groaning and sorrow,—upheld by the firm resolve by increasing in virtue every day,—of frequently doing violence to ones'self;—by fasting, watching,

---
* Luc. vi. 25.

prayers, meditation, study, holy reading, manual labour, abstaining from idle talk, and willingly remaining in secret.

2. All joy that comes not from God, passes quickly away, and leaves the soul stained and wounded.

Words that edify, bring joy to those that hear them; harsh words give pain to our friends; but idle words rob us of the fruit that time would have produced.

Be diligent in doing good; patient in bearing with evil; and thou wilt be happy all the days of thy life: for in both thou wilt continually glorify God.

It seldom happens that a person is not in one or other of these states,—sadness or joy; but happy is he who turns all to good, and who draws profit from adversity.

Whoever loves God, receives

from His hand, the bitter as well as the sweet; and both with equal gratitude. Well and firmly does he stand, who placeth not his hope in himself nor in man, but in God.

CHAP. VI.

ON HEARING AND READING THE DIVINE WORD.

"*Beati, qui audiunt Verbum Dei.*"*

"*Blessed are they who hear the word of God and keep it.*"

1. Worthless are all human consolations if they hinder such as are divine.

When thou hearest the Holy Scripture read, remember it is God who speaketh to thee; humble thy-

* Luc. xi. 28.

self then, and receive His words with a grateful heart.

The truth is not to be despised because of the simplicity and want of learning in him who declares it: for he that leads a good life teacheth well; and he that readeth or lectureth well, is a messenger from God.

A faithful teacher passes over in silence what would be hurtful, proclaims what is profitable, and speaks without pretence or varnish; for pure simple truth always sounds agreeably in the ear.

Subtle discourses are hurtful to simple souls; and those which sooth our vanity often lead the spirit into error.

He who in his discourse, deviates from truth, is the enemy of peace: those who hear him shall hardly avoid scandal.

He that passeth judgment with

discretion is worthy of praise; but he that judges harshly and without mercy, is unworthy of mercy.

He that is of a hasty temper does himself much harm—he often oppresses the innocent, secretly rails at those in power, and openly casts ridicule on all good men.

2. He that is of deceitful lips, abuses the confidence of those that listen to him; therefore his friends shall be few.

Publish not scandal; for it is well to be silent: proclaim the truth; for it is salutary: be modest; for it is reasonable: hurt no one; for it is just: be useful to all; for such is piety: and edify thy neighbour by word and deed; for such is religion.

The prudent man thinks before he acts; changes not unreasonably; speaks with reserve concerning that of which, he is ignorant;

and affirms not lightly what is doubtful.

The silence of the mouth is most profitable to the peace of the heart; but the mouth of the fool is always open and ready for strife.

He that seeks to please God, watches over his heart and lips; and trembles lest he lose the grace of devotion, or give offence to those who love peace.

Fair words, albeit many, fill not the bag; nor shall a blaze of eloquent words sanctify the idle or the proud; but he that doth good shall find good.

CHAP. VII.

ON DIVINE CONSOLATION IN TRIBULATION.

"*Juxta est Dominus his, qui tribulato sunt corde.*"*

"The Lord is nigh unto them that are of a contrite heart."

1. There is no one in this world, howsoever good and pious he may be, who has not some burthen,—some trouble to endure. When therefore thou shalt be in tribulation and sorrow of heart, then art thou with Jesus Christ on the cross. But on the other hand, whenever in the time of prayer, thou art sweetly consoled by the grace of the Holy Spirit, then as it were, art thou raised again from the

* Ps. xxxiii. 19.

dead; coming forth like Christ from the sepulchre; and together with Him thou celebratest the Pasch in newness of life, rejoicing in heart.

When words of harshness or of insult are addressed to thee, then art thou made to drink of the chalice of the Lord, for the welfare of thy soul.

2. Murmur not, but drink the bitter draught of thy salvation in silence and resignation—the Lord himself will be thy sure defence in life and in death. God will never forget thee.

For oh! what is more glorious, than by silence and patience, to close the mouth of him who speaketh evil against thee: following the example of Jesus Christ, who was silent before Pilate, when they brought false witness against Him.*

* Matt. xxvi.

Thou art not better, doubtless, than thy God, who, for the love of thee, was cruelly scourged, mocked and at last put to death by the wicked.

Man knows not how far his virtue and worth may go, till he has been tried in the furnace of tribulation.

Christ has many servants, who willingly come to Him, and seat themselves at His table; but He finds few who would follow Him fasting, into the desert.

3. The true lover of the crucified Jesus refuses not to suffer, and to be persecuted by the wicked; that he may thereby become more conformable to his Saviour, who bowed Himself to the ignominy and scandal of the cross.

Because for him who lives the life of Christ, it is a great gain to suffer and to die for Christ.*

* Phil. i. 21.

The more fervent is thy love for God, the less shalt thou fear death; and the more lively shall be thy desire for the dissolution of the body, that thou mayest live happy with Christ, and share in the joy of His holy angels for all eternity.

Happy is the soul that loveth Jesus tenderly;—in whom the love of eternal good begets contempt for such as pass away;—who endures with patience the evils of this life for the name of Jesus;—who prostrates himself humbly at His feet and begs of Him the grace, to advance still more and more with perseverance and constancy in the paths of virtue.

CHAP. VIII.

ON THE JOY OF A GOOD CONSCIENCE IN THE HOLY SPIRIT.

"*Gaudete in Domino semper.*"*

"*Rejoice in the Lord always.*"

Rejoice together with the good: patiently endure the bad: participate willingly in the sufferings of the afflicted: pardon those who offend thee; and pray for all.

Drive far from thee that gloomy melancholy which begets disgust and rancour in the soul.

Learn the sweet and holy practice of meditating on the life and passion of Jesus Christ; and thou wilt find real consolation both against heaviness of heart and against temptation.

* Phil. iv. 4.

A good life is worthy of praise; but lukewarm conversation is burthensome to all.

A good conscience begets inward joy; but an evil conscience engenders to itself remorse.

Strive always to do well, and thou shalt enjoy lasting peace.

From the malice of the sinner, thou hast nothing to fear, if thou keep steadfast in the path of justice.

Edifying conversation produces joy of heart, and just praise abroad.

Unmerited praise speedily melteth away in the mouth of him who giveth it: for the flattery of a fool is more hurtful than the harsh censure of the wise and just.

2. Humble prayer pierces the heavens, disarms the anger of God, obtains His grace and mercy, and defeats all the artifices of the evil one.

An humble confession deserves forgiveness; but a frivolous excuse aggravates the offence.

Sincere contrition wipes away the stain of sin; and fervent meditation alleviates the penance.

Idle talk weakens the grace of devotion, but pious conversation increases the joy of our soul.

We ought in every place to keep a cautious watch over our senses; and a spiritual retreat is profitable to him whose occupations call him abroad.

Frequent prayer is a sure protection; and the silence of the lips is the secure abode of peace.

Many begin their course with ardour, but those only who persevere unto the end shall obtain the crown of glory.

The yoke of Christ is sweet to those who love; burthensome to the lukewarm; bitter to the proud;

light to the meek, and dear to the humble.

Sweet Jesus maketh all things sweet and light.

The carnal man seeks only the gratification of the senses; but the spiritual man has a horror of such things, and avoids them.

The heaviest affliction of the just man is, that he cannot extinguish in his soul all vicious emotions. But why does God permit their existence? That man may be continually humbled, and may implore the Divine aid unceasingly.

3. Even as the proud man glories in his honours, and the rich in his riches, so he that is truly humble rejoices in self-abasement, and the poor in spirit, in his penury.

Christ, the King of Heaven, is the exceeding glory and riches of the servants of God.

Out of God, all affection is corrupt, all pleasure vain, all abundance poverty.

Nothing, indeed, can satisfy the thirst of the soul, but God alone, Who created it.

The spirit of that man is truly free, which covets none of the things which are of this world.

4. To act well, to suffer evil, to praise God in all things, and never to draw vanity from His good gifts—such is the life of the just.

He that despises himself, and ascribes to God all that he has of good in his thoughts, words, or actions, gives to Him the praise that is truly His due.

When thoughts, then, of vain glory occur to thy mind, consent not to them, but forthwith cry out humbly with the prophet, "Not unto us, O! Lord, not unto us, but to thy name give glory."*

* Ps. cxiii. 1.

Man's most glorious triumph consists in overcoming his affections, in surmounting his dislikes, and in bearing with resignation whatever grievously afflicts him.

CHAP. IX.

ON THE EDIFYING DEMEANOR OF AN HUMBLE BROTHER.

"*Humilibus autem Deus dat gratiam.*"*

"*God giveth grace to the humble.*"

1. A person consecrated to God, ought to be adorned with humility and modesty in all his words and actions, and should never be occupied in trifles.

There is every reason to believe

* Jac. iv. 6.

that a young man engaged in the service of God, will lead a holy life, when, during his novitiate, he practices humility, and speaks little, particularly in the presence of his elders.

He that does not accustom himself to listen, and who learns not to keep silence, will seldom attain a reputation among men of knowledge and wisdom.

Many pass for ignorant, for this only reason, that they are of rude manners.

To obey promptly, to pray frequently, to meditate devoutly, to work diligently, to study cheerfully, to fly the tumult of the world, to love solitude, are the virtues that impart true devotion and inward peace, to souls consecrated to God.

We read in Genesis, "That God had respect to the offerings of Abel, but rejected those of Cain;" and why? because Abel was innocent and humble, Cain envious and perverse.

Be then as Abel, in bearing patiently with everything irksome and grievous; strive not like Cain, lest thou lose the peace of thy soul, and the reputation of a good name. For it is better to lose thy property, than to offend God, to outrage thy brother, and to wound charity.

2. If thou wouldst gain treasure in heaven, cast away the burthen of earth. If thy aim be eternal glory, despise the passing grandeur of this world.

If thou desire peace, beware of the house of contention, and the root of wrath. If thou wouldst be great in heaven, be as a little one on earth.

Seek not to be justified in the eyes of man; for all human praise is delusive, when the witness of a bad conscience accuseth.

The bold and the babbler are alike blame-worthy; both overstep the bounds of rectitude.

Many among the strong have perished, for they presumed too much on their own strength: but many of the weak are strengthened, for they call on the name of the Lord, and put their trust in Him.

The humble and the meek are loved by all—but the stern and severe man is shunned by his neighbours.

The patient and the silent man triumphs over his enemies by condescension and charity.

He that willingly lends his service to others, and sympathizes with them in their sorrows, increases the number of his friends. He that cannot keep silence in season, shall be covered with confusion before many.

3. He that knows how to advance in virtue, to amend himself, and to deserve esteem by the practice of virtue is wise, and possesses true knowledge.

He is strong in power who vigorously resists his vices. He is a sovereign lord who reigns over the depraved affections of his heart He is a brave soldier, and armed at point, who by the arms of continence subdues his flesh :—but he that lives chastely on earth, deserves a place among the angels of heaven.

The chaste man is the friend of God, the companion of angels, the brother of virgins, the beloved fellow-citizen of the saints. He that joins humility to chastity, triumphs over the evil one, while he puts to flight the immodest.

That prelate is truly eminent, who rules over himself with the rod of virtue, and gives a good example to those subject to him.

He that imitates the virtuous is worthy of their praise: and that man is truly noble and free, who is ennobled by virtue.

Fair and comely is he who is unsullied by sin; but howsoever adorned the sinner be outwardly, he still is foul and hideous within.

He that is full of the grace of God, and covets not worldly honours, is both rich and happy; but ignorance and folly is the lot of him who rejects what is beneficial, and embraces what is injurious, to his soul.

To seek the things which are eternal, and to despise such as "perish in the using," —this is divine wisdom.

4. Wise is he who departeth not

from the doctrine of the holy fathers and doctors of the church, and who preserveth in its integrity, the deposit of the faith.

The love of God, and the keeping of His commandments—this is true and honourable wisdom.

If any one apply for instruction, point out to him the path of humility, and walk thyself before him.

He that is truly humble, knows not vanity—disclaims praise—rejoices in contempt—and keeps no place in his memory for wrong or insult.

CHAP. X.

ON THE INSTABILITY OF THE HUMAN HEART.

"*Qui manet in me, et ego in eo, hic fert fructum multum.*"*

"*He that abideth in Me and I in him, the same beareth much fruit.*"

1. The thoughts and affections of man change and vary unceasingly; but all are vain and impure which are not of God.

Oh heart of man! ever too greedy and insatiable! what misery and bitterness is thine in forsaking thy God! why toil after so many empty trifles that can bring thee no consolation nor satisfy thy wants?

What then art thou doing, or

* Joan. xv. 5.

GARDEN OF ROSES. 41

whither dost thou go looking for happiness?

Return, return speedily into thine own heart; see in how many things thou hast offended, and take care to repair the evil thou hast done.

Make ready a dwelling place for thy God; and cast away the rush of vain imaginings, and all external cares, that thou mayest be filled with the consolations of the Holy Spirit.

2. He that often goes abroad is rarely the better for it; for all that glitters so fair in the world, leads to nothing real.

The eye is not satisfied with what it sees; and what strikes the ear filleth not the heart; and if all be not referred to the praise of the Creator, all that thou seest is but an empty vision.

Hence the holy David sings—

"Thou hast given me, O Lord, a delight in Thy doings, and in the works of Thy hands shall I rejoice."*

In no created thing is there any stability; there is nothing permanent or enduring but God, our sovereign good.

Abide in the truth; it will deliver thee from falsehood, from iniquity, and from the malice of thy enemies.

The slander that is falsely circulated against one's neighbour, shall return on the head of the inventor.

Christ is truth; and he that follows Him loves the truth, and all virtue.

He that sacrifices truth to temporal advantage, fortune or honours, makes shipwreck of his faith, and bids adieu to the glory which is the reversion of virtue.

* Ps. xci. 5.

God is truth, and permits not liars to remain long concealed.

The evil doer may for some time disseminate his falsehood, but the truthful man shall at last prevail, and the hypocrite be confounded in the hour he thinks not of.

Let not thy thoughts or thy desires be set on any thing but what is just or pleasing to God; so shalt thou practice virtue, and work good works for the glory of God.

3. He that speaks the truth, and hates iniquity, shall be great in the kingdom of heaven: but he that works iniquity, and hates the truth, shall be tormented with eternal punishment.

Abide in truth and in charity, and thus shalt thou be pleasing to God, to angels, and to men.

Fear not—the wicked may haply deprive thee of some transitory good, but God will grant to him who patiently suffers from injustice, goods that are infinitely greater and eternal.

Dost thou wish thy soul to dwell in peace, and thy conscience to reproach thee in nothing? Be humble, be patient, be obedient—for

There is no enemy so dangerous as thyself, when thy passions are roused.

Look carefully into thy own faults, and thou wilt find little inclination to weigh the actions of others.

CHAP. XI.

ON TRUST IN GOD IN TIME OF TROUBLE.

"*Spera in Domino, et fac bonitatem.*"*

"*Trust in the Lord and do good.*"

1. Let no man glory in the temporal advantages he may enjoy, nor put his trust in friends and familiars: for all things are uncertain, and full of peril: but he that puts his trust in the Lord, and will call upon Him in the time of need, shall not be forsaken in his worst tribulation.

He whose life is good—whose words are edifying—who offends no one—who keeps a strict watch against iniquity, and over his evil

* Ps. xxxvi. 3.

thoughts, shall enjoy much peace. Shut the door of thy house, and thou shalt sleep in peace.

2. He that provides not every day some good thought or edifying action, to oppose as a shield to the attacks of the evil one, shall fall an easy prey to the enemy.

Many cease to pray, and to resist temptations, when all goes not well with them; but virtue is not to be acquired without pain and strife, nor maintained without assiduous care.

A dissipated and inconstant mind abhors discipline and a retired life, as a bird abhors a state of captivity.

Art thou violently tempted or hardly pressed, or mocked, or loaded with confusion?—despair not: reflect forthwith that thy sins justly deserve the censure and despite of men: suffer patiently, and say trustfully, " It is good for me that thou hast humbled me, O Lord, that I may learn Thy justifications."*

In temptation or tribulation, man learns his entire dependence on God; for then he acknowledges his indigence, and feels the grievousness of his defects. He is both an unfaithful and a foolish servant, who makes use of his master's goods to minister to his own vanity, and thence to despise others.

3. He that despises his brethren and fellow servants, or thinks himself better than they, outrages God and all His saints: and the principal cause of this error—is, that we cease to be humble, and cast aside the remembrance of our own faults, while we cease to watch and weep over them.

It is enough for each to bear his

* Ps. cxviii. 71.

own burthen; why then do we busy ourselves, intermeddling with the conduct of others? Why charge ourselves with a burthen heavier than we can bear?

It sometimes happens that a man's faults, errors, and negligences become public, in order to teach him more humility, and more compassion towards the weaknesses of his brethren, and to dispose him to guide with all charity into the way of peace, those who err. Taught by his own experience he says,—" This is a man, and not an angel; it has happened to him, as it has already happened to me; we are brethren—my intentions were bad, and his may perhaps have been good. He who has never erred, nor ever done wrong, is God alone.

Why mockest thou when thy brother falls? " Let him that

thinketh himself to stand, take heed lest he fall."* Is thine own fall a cause of mockery?

The shame of an open fall often entirely extinguishes all emotions of vain glory.

CHAP. XII.

ON THE EFFICACY OF PRAYER, AND THE ADVANTAGES OF PIOUS READING.

" *Sine intermissione orate.*"†

"*Pray without ceasing.*"—*And why? Because we are girt about by tribulations and temptations; by the snares and suggestions of bad angels.*

1. Tidings of good come rarely; war pervades all; fear within:

* 1 Cor. x. 12. † 1 Thess. v. 17.

combat without: there is no day free from toil or trouble, no hour without the dreadful apprehension of death.

By the just judgment of God, are nations ravaged by fire and sword. By these scourges He punishes the crimes of the wicked, and leadeth His elect to seek for eternal blessings.

Unceasing prayer, then, is of the highest importance, not only against the dangers of the world, but as a breastplate, proof against the fiery darts of the enemy.

He that ceases to pray, abandons the conflict; and he that strives not in battle, is already overcome, and has lost the crown of victory.

But, who can pray always? and fight always?

All things are possible to him that calls on the Lord, and puts his trust in him; for "the Lord is nigh unto all that call upon Him,—to all that call upon Him in truth."*

If thou canst not pray always with the lips, pray with the spirit, and in the heart; pray by the fervour of thy desires, and the purity of thy intentions.

A firm desire to do good, and to serve God, is a continual sacrifice offered to Him on the altar of our hearts; for he "prays without ceasing," who never ceases to do well.

He that mourns over his past transgressions, and who sighs for farther growth in virtue, "prays without ceasing." Say then with holy David:—"Lord, all my desire is before Thee and my groaning is not hidden from Thee."*

2. The word of God and pious

* Ps. cxliv. 18.   * Ps. xxxvii. 10.

reading are most useful to recal and calm our spirit, when distracted by external cares, or by some passion from within, that would domineer over it.

Pious reading teaches us the right path of life; good examples excite our imitation, and prayer obtains from heaven the needful grace to follow them.

Reading *of* God is good; praying *to* God is better; but prayer *for* God, is the best of all.

Blessed is he, who in all his words and actions, proposes to himself no other end than the glory of God; desiring that in all and above all, He may be praised and blessed forever.

3. How can a religious man be called devout? or how can he become so, if he prefer idle babbling before reading, study, and prayer?

He that takes pleasure in speaking or listening to, frivolous things, barters his soul for a pitiful price.

In all temptation or tribulation, fly to prayer, as to the secure harbour of thy soul:—humbly imploring the divine assistance. The more readily thou wilt have recourse to it, the more efficacious will it be. The more thou delayest, the less advantage shalt thou obtain: the more frequent it be, the more profit wilt thou draw from it: the more fervent it be, the more pleasing to God.

God, who is good and merciful, loves us to ask of Him: He furnishes us with occasions for prayer, and He hath promised that we shall be heard; since he hath said, "Ask and it shall be given unto you."*

He invites us to prayer by His discourses,—leads us thither by

* Matt. vii. 7.

His example,—constrains us by His threats and encourages us by His favours:—He punishes our negligence by adversity;—rewards our submission, by prosperity; and in this *evening* and *morning* of pains and consolations, is our *one day* of life accomplished.*

Moreover, God often communicates to those who pray devoutly,—who love retreat and silence, interior consolations, which he refuses to those who love the world, and its idle conversation.

4. But ye who love good tidings, come and entertain yourselves with Jesus Christ; listening to Him as He speaks of the kingdom of God,—of the judgment to come,—of the Heavenly Jerusalem,—of the happiness which the inhabitants of heaven, the orders and choirs of angels, enjoy,—of the glory and

† Gen. i.

honour of the elect, and of the recompense of the saints, exulting in joy and gladness for all eternity.

Hearken to the prophets announcing the hidden mysteries of Christ, and thundering with the divine vengeance against the unrepentant sinner.

Listen to the apostles and evangelists, as they publish abroad the wonderful works and miracles of Jesus Christ.

Listen to the doctors of the Church, as they speak with eloquent tongues of holy things, and explain what is obscure in the Scriptures; adorning their lives by the splendour of their virtues, and refuting heresy and schism by the solidity of their reasoning.

May each one of us choose in these instructions, the truths most suited to our taste or wants. Let us not pass over with disdain such as seem simple, nor censure those which are above our intellect: for it is folly to reprove the wise; but it is impiety to condemn the saints and men inspired of God.

5. Labour steadfastly then to learn first the most simple truths, and humbly resolve to practice the least, however small; and if it be to thy advantage, God will soon impart a knowledge of higher mysteries: for it is written: "To him who knoweth to do good, and doth it not, to him it is sin."*

He that is stored with knowledge, and makes not use of it to regulate his conduct; and he that reads, but profits not by what he reads, are like those who go away empty and famished, from a table that is abundantly spread.

As he that works little, shall be

* Jas. iv. 17.

long in want; so he that seldom prays, shall be long lukewarm.

He that discourses against vice in others and corrects not his own, scatters good seed among thorns: and little fruit will be gathered from many words, if one comes to prayer without first casting out his evil thoughts.

Happy is he that with earnest care, casts forth from his soul all impurity; suffering nothing to remain in the secret of his heart, that can offend in secret the eyes of God.

By an humble confession of sins, a soul humble and contrite before God, is purified from all vices.

6. The pious man finds pleasure in prayer; the studious man in his books; the devout soul, in the practice of virtue; the proud, in honours; the humble, in contempt; the rich, in his riches; the beggar,

in his alms; the glutton, in eating and drinking: the idle in frivolous talk; the abstemious man, in temperance; the wise, in wisdom; the good monk, in submission to his rule;—but none of these enjoyments are to be compared with those which flow from the love of God, and the peace of a good conscience.

Wouldst thou triumph over the enemies most dangerous to thy soul?—have recourse to flight—to silence—to solitude—to prayer—to fasting—to study—to labour.

A holy man thinks on holy things, speaks the truth, and acts justly; despises things present, and meditates on those that are eternal.

The humble man receives the advice that is given to him; the prudent man avoids danger; the patient suffers with resignation; the diligent neglects not his occupation; and he that shuns not small faults, shall fall into great ones.

7. He that is lukewarm in the morning, will rarely be found fervent at the close of the day.

He that promptly shakes off slothful torpidity and forthwith betakes himself to labour, acquires thereby great inward satisfaction, and honour; although he may not be recompensed by men, he certainly will by God: which is far better and infinitely more to be prized by all. For God giveth Himself to the saints, to be their reward and the eternal recompense of their good works, their toils, and their sufferings.

The idle man is never satisfied with the idle frivolities of the world, but the virtuous man denies himself even of things that are lawful.

He that makes humility, the foundation of all his actions, and counts as nothing the honours of this world, shall walk with an assured step in the way that is good.

The wisest of men is he, and wisely doth he live, who studies to please God alone, who disengages himself from exterior objects and attaches himself to interior things only; who despises every thing which is of earth, and aspires to the glories of heaven alone;— who ever prefers the love of God to all the goods of this world.

CHAP. XIII.

ON THE PRAISES OF CHARITY, AND ITS FRUITS.

"*Omnia vestra in charitate fiant.*"*

"*Let all your actions be done in charity.*"

1. Charity is a noble virtue, and surpasses all virtues, knowledge and gifts. Charity embraces God Himself; it unites angels to men; it elevates the children of men to the dignity of children of God, and friends of the saints. Hence also did Christ condescend to be born of a virgin, and to be crucified for the salvation of the human race.

Charity purifies the soul from sin; it warms and inflames, and fills us with a wondrous sweet-

* 1 Cor. xvi. 14.

ness, making us love God, with all our heart, with all our mind, and with all our strength.

It justifies the sinner, and sets the bond-slave free; of an enemy it makes a friend; of a foreigner, a fellow-citizen; of a stranger, a familiar. It teaches the inconstant, constancy; the proud, humility; the perverse, meekness: it gives to the lukewarm, fervour; to the broken heart it brings joy; it opens the hand of the avaricious; it awakes the worldly man to spiritual life; it gives wisdom and knowledge to the ignorant. Such are the effects of charity when it comes into the soul of the faithful, through the Holy Spirit, which is given to them from heaven.

Its flight is bold and daring, for it rises above the Cherubim and Seraphim, and all the angelic choirs.

It comprehends both the means and the extremes; forming but one and the same whole of things most opposite.

It infuses joy into the heart of all men—of one and all—not that joy which has its foundation in personal complacency, but that which maketh glad the heart, whose every affection is for God.

Charity pervades both heaven and earth, sea and land;—all that the eye can see or ear can hear of the wonders of creation, it refers to the praise and glory of the Creator.

Throughout all nature there is not anything, howsoever small or contemptible, which, by the perfection of its being, reveals not the hand of its Sovereign Maker, the power of the Creator, the wisdom of the Disposer, and the providence of Him who rules and governs all supremely well: and this consideration leads the devout soul to praise God, to bless Him and celebrate His praises, at all times, and in every place.

As wax melts before the fire, so by charity the soul is kindled inwardly: it ceases to be chained to earth; then mounting upwards, it soars above the stars of heaven, to seek the only object of its love,—God, the Creator and Ruler of all things: in whom it can repose in absolute security, and rejoice in perfect beatitude.

2. Oh, what sweetness and happiness does he taste, who is joined with God, and inwardly rejoices in Him!

Oh! how happy should we be, if we could taste but a little of that eternal blessedness, which appears unclouded to the angels forever.

But alas! we are recalled from

these soaring aspirations, to an active life, and are obliged to fight courageously with the arms of charity, against the temptations which daily assault us.

For oftentimes after joy comes affliction; after consolation, sadness; after laughing, weeping; after peace and repose, inward war and trouble of soul:—great consolations are often succeeded by profound desolation, or by a troublesome temptation, or a corporal infirmity, or some human contrariety, or the loss of friends, or the assaults of our enemies, or trouble of soul, or the railleries of the younger, the censure of the old, or the severe reproof of our superiors.

All these things are sent to humble the pride of our hearts; or to make us show compassion to the weaknesses of others, or to such as are in temptation or affliction.

Let us not then trust in ourselves, nor be over wise, nor look to our own advantage; but let us humble ourselves to all, being subject to God, and to every creature for God's sake.* Such is true charity.

By charity God came down into the world: by charity were the gates of heaven re-opened to man.

By charity, Christ came down to save sinners. By charity and the ignominy of the cross, He ascended to the right-hand of His Father, and thus assured to man the highest of honours.

3. Charity is never idle; for it is busied with things the highest and the most exalted: it also descends graciously and willingly to the humble and lowly.

* 1 Pet. ii. 13.

It labours with diligence in honourable callings, and it delights in the meanest employment that obedience imposes.

It shows no repugnance to clean the wounds of the sick, to wash their feet, to make their beds, to clean their clothes, or sweep up their filth.

It suffers in patience, and rejoices in the midst of reproach and evil speaking.

4. As fire burns faggots, so the fire of charity consumes the fuel of vice. It purifies the heart by contrition,—washes it by confession,—cleanses it by prayer,—enlightens it by holy reading,—inflames it by devout meditation,—fosters it by holy retirement, and unites it to God, by the fervour of its love.

Charity excites the mouth of man to sing the praises of God,—his hands to labour for Him,—his feet to walk in his service,—his eyes to contemplate His glories,—his memory to recal His benefits,—all his body to minister to Him, and all his faculties to love God above all that is in heaven or on earth.

Charity, when joined with humility, repairs the past ravages of sin,—fortifies it against future dangers,—gives it discernment of things present,—delivers it from many doubts,—sets a guard against curiosity,—retrenches all superfluities,—casts aside all vain things; discovers such as are false,—inspires horror of such as are shameful,—softens what is hard,—gives understanding of things obscure,—reveals in prayer the secrets of heaven; and, in a word, governs all, within and without.

Charity, in a holy soul, is that prompt good will which ceases not to work for God; although the weakness of human nature, and imperious circumstances, permit it not always to realize the good intended.

5. Happy is the pure soul, to whom God is all; who feels no pleasantness nor worth out of God, and who sees nothing that deserves its affection—yea, rather, all bitter and burthensome. Such is the soul God seeks, such is the soul God loves; because for His love it has despised and renounced all, even its own affections, and because it fights courageously to preserve its purity.

Free from all earthly affection, the pure soul springs forth swiftly, and impatient of all control, and above created worlds, to lose itself in the bosom of its God.

Charity breaks all bonds that chain it to the world: makes light its heavy burthens, and hastens to fulfil with faithfulness whatever is pleasing to God. Whence it prays with Christ, its divine model, saying: "Father, not my will but Thine, always and every where, be done, Amen."*

CHAP. XIV.

ON WATCHING AND STRIVING AGAINST TEMPTATIONS.

"*Resistite diabolo, et fugiet a vobis.*"†

"*Resist the devil, and he will fly from you.*"

1. Wherever the just man unites his soul to God, by prayer, by meditation, by study, by writing,

---

* Matt. xxvi. 39.   † Jac. iv. 7.

or any other useful labour; there are on one side holy angels who rejoice with him, and on the other, evil spirits who send distractions and temptations.

When thou beginest to pray, the devils take to flight, as from the fire of the Holy Spirit; but when thou wilt begin to indulge in frivolous idle talk, they quickly return to excite and increase thy distraction.

But a good and watchful superior, prudently interposing, will put an end to all idle conversation; reprove those who waste the precious hours, and neglect good works.

Dwell then in silence, and let God be in all thy thoughts, and all thy consolations, and thou wilt find no longer that disrelish for good works, which hinders thee from pursuing with ardour, thy holy enterprise.

2. Be faithful in little things, and thou shalt be rewarded with talents beyond measure, in the kingdom of heaven.

Be neither idle in solitude, nor a babbler in public, and the evil one, overcome by thy diligence and silence, shall depart; for he loves not a man who works and maintains silence,—who loves prayer and holy meditation.

Wherever thou art, alone, or in company, it is indispensable to fight, to watch, and to pray against the temptations of the flesh and the spirit.

Fight valiantly, pray with fervour, perform thy work with diligence, study often, love silence, and suffer patiently. Put all thy trust in God, how great soever the tribulations or desolation may be, that are sent for thy trial.

He that learns in every place,

and at all times, to practice patience, shall overcome his enemies, and enjoy in this world a peace which knows no change, and in the world to come, a brighter crown of glory with the elect.

CHAP. XV.

ON BEARING ONE ANOTHER'S BURTHENS.

"*Alter alterius onera portate.*"*

"*Bear ye one another's burdens.*"

1. As we all are but one body in Christ, so we ought to preserve fraternal charity, knit together in the bond of peace; and ever be united in the pursuit of virtue.

* Gal. vi. 2.

We are all members of Christ, regenerated in baptism, by the grace of the Holy Spirit; redeemed by the passion of Christ; purified by the blood of Christ; fed by the body of Christ; instructed by the words of Christ; confirmed by the miracles of Christ; and led to virtue by the example of Christ; why then, my brethren, would ye seek to hurt one another?

He that offers an affront to his brother, be it in word or deed, offers an affront to Christ; and He shall avenge and punish the wrong, if the offender shall not speedily repair the injury and atone for his conduct.

We all have God for our Father in Heaven; we are consequently all brethren in Christ; whatever be the country or kindred whence we are collected here below, and whether we be of obscure or of noble blood.

One God hath made us all; it is the same God who preserves and governs us; it is the same God who called us,—who still daily calls us by His word from without, by contrition from within, to the same beatitude. It is the same God, who promises to manifest Himself eternally to us, in the presence of His angels, and to be our eternal recompense, in the harmonious blessedness of all the inhabitants of the heavenly kingdom.

If, therefore, we are all called by the same God, redeemed by the same price, imbued and sanctified by the same spirit, let it be our constant endeavour to love and serve one another.

If we would be pleasing to Christ, " let us bear one another's burthens," for Christ's love; and let us pray one for another in charity, for God is equally in each of us, and each of us in Him.

Whatever imperfection or folly we observe in our brethren, we ought charitably and considerately to excuse them, as we would that they would excuse us.

2. Beloved brother, bear with others, and they will bear with thee; excuse, and thou wilt be excused; pity the weaknesses of the sinner, and thou wilt be pitied; comfort him that is afflicted, and thou shalt be comforted by him that is in joy; raise up him that falls, and thou shalt be raised up by the help of God.

As thou wilt have done to another, so also shall it be done unto thee, by the just and terrible retribution of God.

Be not astonished, nor indignant, if man, who is frail, fall in this world; angels fell in heaven; and Adam, in the earthly paradise, overcome by the attraction of a pitiful apple.

A very little thing often tempts a man violently: and a trifle that hardly deserves notice, often grievously affects him. God justly permits this to be so, to teach us that if we do not resist small trials, we cannot overcome great ones.

3. Be full of indulgence and kindness to thy brother when he is tempted; and pray for him when he is in tribulation, as for thyself.

The good which happens to thee, becomes mine, when I rejoice with thee for it; and thy misfortunes are mine, when I sympathize with thee in them; for all men are frail, and therefore it is the duty of all charitably to pray one for another.

We must not upbraid others with defects, and despise them for such, when we overlook the like in ourselves; for it would be as a blind man mocking the blind, or the deaf, him that cannot hear, or a fool that laughs at a fool.

Never speak to the disadvantage of one over whose conduct thou hast no charge; look rather to thyself, and repair the evil thou findest there.

If thy intention be good, and thou really mean to correct the faults of thy brother, begin by correcting thy own; thou mayest then proceed to the reformation of his, not with ill natured or over heated zeal, but with prudence and modesty.

If thou lovest me sincerely, and with a brother's affection, be as indulgent to me as thou art to thyself, and pray for me.

He that would correct his brother, and thinks that he is dispensed with praying for him, and excused from having compassion for his infirmities, is neither a kind-hearted nor a sensible physician, but a cruel enemy and a burthensome railer.

He that prays for others, as well as for himself, does two good actions.

The more deeply thou art penetrated with just sentiments of fraternal charity, the more cheerfully and promptly wilt thou pray for thy brother, asking God to grant him grace to amend, and to cease to be a scandal to the weak : so the deeper will thy sorrow be, if he refuse to listen, or if he take thy warnings ill.

For each one is to his brother,

either a fragrant rose, or a troublesome thorn.

CHAP. XVI.

ON THE LOVE OF CHRIST, AND HATRED OF THE WORLD.

"*Mane in dilectione meâ.*"*

"*Abide in my love.*"

1. These are the words of our Lord and Saviour Jesus Christ: sweet is the voice of Christ unto the hearing, and salutary unto obedience for all.

The love of Christ is the joy of the mind, and the paradise of the soul; it shuts out the world, and overcomes the devil; it closes the mouth of hell, and opens wide the gates of heaven.

* Joan, xv. 9.

The love of Christ, and the love of the world, are contrary, the one to the other, and have nothing in common; nor can they dwell together.

The love of Christ, like the chariot of Elias, carries the soul up to heaven; but the love of the world like the conveyance of Satan, drags it down to hell. Self-love is like that of a suicide; it is self-destruction:—the total forgetfulness of the world conducts to the certain discovery of heaven.

The flattering words of a false friend, are more hurtful than the harsh reproof of the just.

The imagination of the deceitful invents falsehood; but the spirit of the just man seeks truth at the fountain head.

He that scandalizes his brother, shall himself be scandalized.

God, who knoweth and ruleth

over all, suffereth not His poor sheep to wander long, or to fill the air with empty bleatings; but either by the correcting staff of fear, leads back the strayed one to the fold, or looking down on it with the eyes of love, sweetly guides it home by the interior voice of conscience.

2. Where peace and concord dwell together, there is God, and with Him all good.

Where strife and dissension dwell together, there is the devil and with him all evil.

"Where pride is, there also is the root of all evil; but where humility is, there also is wisdom."*

Trample pride under foot, and thou shalt find much peace.

Where harsh and wrangling words are heard, the bowels of charity are wounded.

* Prov. xi. 2.

Where solitude and silence reign, there persons devoted to God, find repose.

Where strict discipline and the love of labour prevail, religious souls make rapid progress in virtue. Where laughter and dissipation meet, the sweets of devotion take wings and fly away, for the idler and the babbler are seldom contrite, and rarely free from sin.

Where obedience is ready, the conscience is joyful: but where frivolous conversation is prolonged, work is neglected.

Where there is overmuch delicacy or self-seeking, there, is charity defective or cold: where the doctrine of Christ flourishes, the path of salvation is made secure.

Where brethren dwell together in unity, there, sounds the most harmonious rise to heaven.

Where moderation is observed,

the virtue of concord shall last the longer.

Where those who offend are reproved with prudence and moderation, no one can justly complain, or accuse his superior : whence some one hath said, " In all things be moderate, for moderation is a most seemly virtue."

Where patience dwells, a great enemy is overcome; but where disquiet or disorder enters, peace soon takes its departure.

Put a guard on the entrance of thy mouth, and weigh well thy words before giving them utterance.

Where faith and truth meet together, peace dwells secure; but with fraud and iniquity, foolish imaginings and bootless prudence alone shall be thy guests.

Where charity is, there is the Holy Spirit.

Where the disposition is mistrustful, there will be no lack of fuel for anger and strife; but where there is the knowledge of the truth, there will be joy to the upright of heart.

Under a deceitful tongue often skulks a false friend; the humble confession of a fault obtains a ready pardon.

When the wisdom of man can do nothing, it is then that we must implore with more earnestness the divine protection.

He that makes choice of the way of malice and injustice, shall come to an evil end; but peace in abundance shall light upon him, who follows the footsteps of virtue, and who strives to be patient.

Woe to the impious man who does evil: woe to the hypocrite who seems to do good: because none shall suffer more than themselves from their iniquity.

"A double-minded man is inconstant in all his ways,"* and very wicked; but blessed is the simple and the just, in whom there is no guile: for God is with him assisting him in all his works, and guiding his feet into the right path.

When a man has once been faithless to his word, who shall lightly trust him? but he that changes his former opinion for a better, breaks not the word of truth.

3. It is pleasant to listen to the recital of acts of virtue, but it is still more praiseworthy to put them in practice.

The best examination of conscience is that which leads to a change of life; and the fruits of a good examination are, abstaining from sin, and advancement in virtue.

* Jas. i. 8.

The worthy fruits of devout prayer, is the union of the heart with God, in the fervour of the Holy Spirit: he prays devoutly who drives away all frivolous thoughts.

He that places before him the image of the crucifix, shall drive away the illusions of the devil; and that soul has a most salutary employment, which meditates continually on the passion of Christ.

He that meditates daily on the sacred wounds of Jesus, pours a healing and a cleansing balm on the wounds of his own soul.

He that utterly despises the goods of this world as mere dirt, and thirsts not after its honours, shall obtain purity of heart, and shall without hindrance give himself up to the service of God.

He that would give perfect praise and honour to God, will

practice profound humility of heart, and constantly meditate, groan, and weep over all his defects.

The sincere and humble contrition of a sinner is like a powerful voice, which penetrates to the ear of God.

4. Whatever good you do, do all to the glory of God.

He tramples under foot, and wounds to death, all pride, envy, and vain glory, who refers simply, purely, and wholly, to the honour and glory of God, all the virtues which he practices, as well as all the good works of others; ascribing everything to God, and attributing nothing to his own merits, nor to his own strength, but stripping himself of all, acknowledges God as the first author of all that is good. That man renounces eternal honour who takes complacency and glory in himself, and not in

God alone, who is the sovereign good.

And thus it was that the blessed Virgin Mary, when she sought to express the delight of her heart, for the inestimable benefits she had received from her Creator, exclaimed in her sublime Canticle: "My spirit hath rejoiced in God my Saviour."*

"If any man think himself to be something, whereas he is nothing, he deceives himself," saith St. Paul the Apostle;† who, even though rapt to the third heaven, gloried in nothing of himself, but refered to God alone all the good that he did, whether by his preaching or his writings: "by the grace of God," says he, "I am what I am."‡

* Luke i. 47. † Gal. vi. 31. ‡ 1 Cor. xv. 10.

CHAP. XVII.

ON THE IMITATION OF THE MOST HOLY LIFE OF OUR LORD JESUS CHRIST.

"*Quamdiu fecisti uni ex his fratribus meis minimis, mihi fecistis.*"*

"*As long as you did it to one of these, my least brethren, you did it to me.*"

1. Note these words,—weigh well the mysteries they contain, and let them be unto thee as a rule of life.

He that comforts a brother in distress, stretches out his hand to Jesus.

He that bears with patience the burthen which Providence has laid

* Matt. xxv. 40.

on him, carries on his shoulders Jesus, and Him crucified.

He that addresses words of consolation to the afflicted, gives to Jesus a loving kiss.

He that mourns over the faults of his brother, and supplicates for his pardon, washes and wipes the feet of Jesus.

He that turns the anger of his brother to peace, prepares in his soul a bed of flowers for Jesus.

He that at table gives up to a brother, the better portion set aside for himself, feeds Jesus with the bread and honey of charity.

He that meditates piously and fervently on the adorable perfections of God, introduces Jesus into the secret chamber of his soul.

He that presents a book of holy wisdom to his brother, offers choice wine to the lips of Jesus.

He that prohibits frivolous conversation, drives away the flies from the table of Jesus.

He that will not hearken to detraction, but reproves unseemly conversation, arms himself with a staff to drive away an inauspicious animal from the house of Jesus.

He that during refection reads to his brethren correctly and distinctly, serves up a heavenly cup to the guests of Jesus, and inebriates them with the wine of joy; but he that reads ill, takes away the relish of the food; and he that stammers, stains the cloth which covers tne table of Jesus.

He that hears his neighbour slandered, and feels therefrom much grief and deep sorrow, anoints with balm, the sacred wounds of Jesus.

2. He that speaks of the good example and virtues of his neigh-

bour, presents to Jesus, a nosegay of fair flowers.

He that reads devoutly, and announces piously the words of Jesus, diffuses sweet perfume in the nostrils of those that hear him.

He that bears charitably with the faults of his neighbour, and gives them a favourable construction, shall readily obtain mercy from Jesus.

He that throws a veil over the vices or scandals of his neighbour, spreads a garment over the naked limbs of Jesus.

He that meditates on the humble life and divine miracles of Jesus, and therewith sweetly nourishes his soul, drinks in milk and honey from the mouth of Jesus.

Thus spoke and thus acted the blessed Agnes, who afterwards, had the happiness of shedding her blood for the love of Jesus.

He that reads or sings in the place of a weak or sick brother, sweetly plays on the harp with the angels before the cradle of Jesus.

He that prays devoutly, abstains from delicate meats, and renounces all his possessions, comes with the holy Magi to lay three costly offerings in the hands of the infant Jesus.

He that washes the feet and garments of his brethren, and does the meanest offices, baptizes Jesus, with St. John the Baptist.

He that loves solitude and silence, enters the desert with Jesus.

He that does violence to his inclinations, and chastises his body, fasts with Jesus.

He that speaks words of salvation to his brethren, preaches with Jesus of the kingdom of heaven.

He that prays constantly for

such of his brethren as are weak or in temptation, visits Lazarus with Jesus, and weeps with Martha and Mary at His tomb.

3. He that offers or frequently hears the holy sacrifice of the mass for the faithful departed, or recites the office for them, comes with Jesus to the tomb of Lazarus, to beg that He would mercifully deliver their souls from suffering.

He that goes to the common refectory with his brethren, to hear spiritual reading, eateth and drinketh with Jesus and His disciples.

He that lays up in his heart the words of God, which he has heard in the refectory, reposes with the Apostle St. John, during the last supper, on the breast of Jesus.

He that submits humbly, and without delay, to do what is painful to him, truly follows Jesus with His disciples to Mount Olivet, where he was betrayed and delivered to His enemies.

He that has instant recourse to fervent prayer in tribulation or temptation, contends together with Jesus in His agony, against the assaults of Satan.

He that entirely renounces his own will, fulfils the will of God the Father, with Jesus, and with courageous resignation carries his cross even to Calvary.

He that prays for his enemies, and willingly pardons those that have sinned against him, prays with Jesus that his enemies may not perish, but rather that they may be converted unto God and live.

He that voluntarily renounces the things of this world, and casts aside the flattery of the senses, expires with Jesus on the cross; and his spirit, like that of the Apostle St. Paul, is rapt even to Paradise.

4. He that keeps his heart clean and peaceful, wraps up Jesus in fair white linen, and entombs Him in his breast.

He that perseveres unto the end in the service of Jesus, sweetly reposes with Him in the peaceful slumber of the holy sepulchre.

He that weeps for the sorrows of the blessed Virgin Mary, deserves that she and her holy Son, should console him in his affliction, and last agony.

He that in spirit recalls the words and actions of Jesus, and makes thereof a spiritual food, prepares sweet spikenard to soften the bitterness of his passion.

He that gives humble and devout thanks for the blessings he has received, comes with Mary Magdalen, bringing sweet perfume to the sepulchre of Jesus.

He that after contrition and confession of sins, firmly resolves to amend his life, rises with Jesus from the death of sin.

He that shakes off his spiritual torpor and lukewarmness, and becomes animated with new fervour, celebrates in spirit a new pasch with Jesus, and sings with Him in choir a hallelujah of joy.

He that despises the pleasures of the world,—flies from its dangers,—loves a religious life, and accepts its obligations, enters with Jesus and his disciples into "the upper chamber," there to serve God in freedom and in secret; there to lead a life more pure, and to receive more abundantly the graces of the Holy Spirit.

He that is cold and indifferent on earthly things, and enflamed through holy meditation, with such as are heavenly, forsakes the earth with Jesus, and mounts with Him to heaven.

Blessed is the soul in which " to live is Christ, and to die is gain,"* for he that would live to Christ, must die to himself: and he that would be wise and happy in the sweetness of Christ, must renounce all perishable things.

Total separation from the things of this world, is painful, and death is grievous: but to reign in joy with Christ, is salvation and life eternal.

Oh! when shall the moment come when God shall be my all?—when I shall be all for Him!—when I shall be united to Him!

For ah! the faithful soul cannot be fully blessed, till it be united to God in glory.

Guided then by divine love, follow Jesus all the days of thy life;

* Phil. i. 21.

filled with a lively faith and animated with an ardent charity:—that thou mayst at length be found worthy to see Him face to face, there, where he is Himself, the blessing and the joy of the angels.

To which beatific vision may Jesus Christ our Lord lead us hereafter:—He who, for us, endured the bitter death of the cross. Amen.

CHAP. XVIII.

ON THE ETERNAL PRAISE OF GOD.

"*Semper laus ejus in ore meo.*"*

"*His praise shall be always in my mouth.*"

1. Oh! words full of sweetness in the ears of all devout christians!

* Ps. xxxiii. 1

but sweeter far when uttered in the high court of heaven in presence of the Almighty King, and His blessed ministers, the holy angels. Were all the instruments of music in the world brought together, in concert and not resound with the praises of their God, vain would be their melody: to a pious soul, they could afford neither pleasure nor satisfaction: because God and His glory must be the prime source of all our music, and not the gratification of miserable vanity: for thus only can our praise be grateful or acceptable to God. When thy songs are animated with pure intentions, then canst thou exult in transports of holy joy with blessed Mary in her sublime canticle. Sweet is the symphony both on earth and in heaven, to praise the Lord, with heart undefiled, and voice in harmony with all creation, for His goodness unspeakable, and glorious magnificence. Delightful task to praise God at all times, to love the Creator of heaven and earth, and to honour abundantly the Giver of eternal life! So indeed the life, the honour, the glory of the holy angels are entirely expended in praising God with all their powers; never ceasing from their song divine: in this, they never tire in singing forth His praise, nor ever praise in vain.

In this manner are the souls of the saints incessantly occupied in their heavenly abodes:—now freed from the chains of the body, and secure from the wiles of Satan and all temptation: united to God in perfect charity, and filled with never ending joy, and happiness unspeakable. Now at rest from all their labours, they look back with infinite delight at the severe trials, the grievous afflictions endured in this life:—at the various dangers and temptations, from which they have escaped. Now all their groans and lamentations are changed into canticles of joy, while the stripes and buffetings inflicted by a vile world, are become a greater augmentation to their crown of glory.

2. Oh! happy country, where all is peace, where grief or sadness is unknown, where everything is refulgent with joy, ever resounding with praise divine and sweetest melody. Therefore praise thou also faithful soul, praise the Lord of heaven; and do thou, O Sion, bending under the load of terrene and grovelling propensities,—do thou praise thy God! Do thou invoke Jesus from the scene of thy conflict;—that attended by His holy angels He may descend to thy

aid, and shield thee by His powerful protection. Beseech him that the power of the evil one may not prevail against thee,—that the wickedness of the flesh may not seduce thee,—that neither the salutary strictness of religious discipline nor the severity of thy necessary labours may overcome thee. For the sake of thy Saviour, cheerfully undergo the burthen of the holy cross, which will hereafter open unto thee the gate of the heavenly kingdom. What wilt thou more?

The royal road leading to Christ, is, to conquer thy headstrong will, —to patiently bear the weakness of thy brother,—and mortify thy flesh. For a transient toil, thou wilt exchange eternal repose;—for an humble state and low degree, thou shalt enjoy honour and glory without end. Let the praise of God therefore, be always in thy mouth, both in prosperity and adversity: for in this, there is abundant merit, if thou resign thyself with all sincerity to the will of God. Whatsoever affliction may happen, whether from within or from without, receive all with humble thankfulness from the hand of a most clement and merciful God who hath care for all His creatures high and low.

He who hath made thee according to His own image and likeness, will not according to his unspeakable goodness, forsake thee in thy necessity.

3. Open then thy mouth to sing the praise of the Omnipotent, by whose providence are directed and governed all things whether in heaven or on earth, in the sea, or the uttermost depths of the abyss. Praise thy Creator who hath made

thee a man and not a beast: and although He had even made thee a fly, still would He merit thy praise as having done well. A lion may not boast of his strength over the fly or the gnat; because although he can make the forests ring with a louder roar, the tiny insect can take a loftier flight.

Let no contention then take place between the great and the small,—between the rich and the poor,—the strong and the weak,—the man of wisdom and the simple of heart,—between the prince and the peasant; but let all with one accord, praise the Lord our God: who hath formed every creature of surpassing beauty and wonderful variety, in order to more abundantly and openly proclaim the honour and glory of His holy name and the benefit of man. O! faithful soul, praise thy merciful Redeemer, who by His death and passion, and sufferings on the cross, hath rescued thee from the sentence of eternal death. Him thou couldst not praise in a manner worthy of these benefits, even if thou couldst endure for His sake, a thousand deaths on a cross. Praise thy Protector who hath preserved thee from so many dangers, and so many sins: praise thy Benefactor who hath bestowed so many benefits as cannot be enumerated. Behold still more,—He daily showers down new favours, and *descends* to thee in person on the holy altar; by which He communicates unto thee, the most precious gift even He can bestow,—HIMSELF; and for all these inestimable favours, He requires nothing more, He esteems nothing more than this,—that with all purity and sincerity, with all thy heart and all thy soul, thou wouldst love and praise Him for His own sake.

4. When thou wilt have experienced much joy and when things have gone well with thee, offer thy praises and thanksgiving, because God in His mercy hath vouchsafed to send thee consolation, lest thou faint on the way: for as often as thou hearest or readest the word of God, as often as thou dost meditate piously and devoutly on the Incarnation or Passion of Christ, so often doth the Lord send bread from heaven to cheer and comfort thy soul. When on the other hand, thou shalt have been overtaken with sadness or surprised with weakness, offer thy praises and thanksgiving: because God then visits, tries, and purifies thee lest thou become puffed up or presume too much on thyself; for, affliction of body is not unfrequently a salu-

salutary recal to compunction of heart.

When thou wilt have been favoured with health of mind and strength of body, then shalt thou offer up praise and thanksgiving, because God hath vouchsafed thee these powers of mind and body, in order that thou mayest give thyself to useful labour or the service of others; never wasting thy valuable hours in idleness.

Whenever thou art in a garden or orchard, on beholding the various kinds of trees, the beautiful flowers and fragrant roses, delicious apples, and mellow pears, the verdant plants and odoriferous lilies, offer up thy praise and thanksgiving, because God deigns to show thee so many of his wondrous works, springing and budding forth from the earth: all of which in admirable power and wisdom, He renews from year to year, in accordance with His benignity and for man's use and benefit.

Therefore at all times and in every place, praise the Lord and give Him thanks because all the earth is filled with His majesty, and His glory is above the heavens. Together with all the saints upon earth, do thou praise the Lord, Who is praised without end, by all the Angels in heaven. In praising God thou art made like unto Angels; in neglecting His praise, thou art base and ungrateful;—yea, worse than the brute beasts.

Behold the birds of the air, how they sing, the fishes of the sea, how they swim, the dogs of the earth, how they bark, the cattle and flocks of the field, how they bleat and low;—all these, each in its way, show forth the praise and glory of God: nay, more the very elements themselves are moved, elevated, and affected with the glory of God, and by their natural motions and regular changes, proclaim the magnificence of their Creator.

Therefore in all thy actions, have God ever before thy eyes; carefully avoiding aught that may offend Him. Thank Him for all the benefits so abundantly bestowed; and at the conclusion of every business and every employment, thus pour out thy liveliest gratitude from the bottom of thy soul,—repeating,—" Praise be to God now and forever more! Let every spirit praise the Lord! Amen."

THE END

OF

THE LITTLE GARDEN OF ROSES.

THE
Valley of Lilies.

THE PROLOGUE

TO THIS LITTLE BOOK.

"*Justus germinabit sicut lilium, et florebit in æternum ante Dominum.*"*

"*The just shall spring as the lily, and his root shall spread forth before the Lord for ever.*"

This little book may be called the *Valley of Lilies*, to distinguish it from that which precedes it, under the title of the *Little Garden of Roses;* for as that treats of many virtues, which spring forth as fair *roses*, in the Garden of *Jesus*, so this discourses of many other virtues, which as so many *lilies* of exceeding whiteness, are planted by our Lord Jesus in the valley of humility ; where they are sweetly bedewed and fertilized by the inward infusion of the Holy Spirit. For, according to the

* Osee xiv. 6.

testimony of St. Gregory, to seek to acquire all other virtues, without humility, is to carry dust against the wind.

It is of these lilies that the spouse of Christ, out of the humility and devotion of her soul, speaketh, in the Canticle of Canticles, when wishing to declare the inward joy and consolation she experienced from the visit of the Divine Spouse, and the graces He had heaped upon her, she says: "I to my beloved, and my beloved to me, who feedeth among the lilies."* And again: "My beloved is white and ruddy." "So shall he repose upon my bosom."

To Him be praise, honour, and glory, for ever and ever. Amen.

* Cant. vi. 2.—v. 10.

THE VALLEY OF LILIES.

CHAP. I.

ON THE THREE-FOLD STATE OF HUMAN LIFE.

"*Ego flos campi, et lilium convallium.*"*

"*I am the flower of the field, and the lily of the valleys.*"

1. This is the voice of Christ, to his holy Church in general, and to every devout soul in particular; for Christ is the goodly and sovereign Spouse of the Church, and the head of all the faithful. He is the

---

* Cant. Cantic. ii. 1.

flower of all virtues, the lily of the valleys, the lover of humility and chastity.

If thou wouldst serve Christ, and please the Heavenly Spouse, overcome thy passions, gather the lilies of virtue, eschew idleness, study diligently, work at some useful manual labour, pray often for a more intimate union with God, turn away from the turmoil of the world, love retirement, and avoid all idle or hurtful conversation.

2. If virtue be not in thy heart, how seemly soever the outward habit, it is worth nothing in the sight of God. The vessel may be of fair proportions outwardly, but within it is empty.

Even as a vessel filled with good wine, exhales a pleasing odour, so from the good heart of a religious man, whose affections are pure, spring forth holy words and edifying works, which contribute to the glory of God, and the profit of his neighbour.

Weigh well then, my brother, the great importance of the state in which thou art engaged, the outward marks of which thou bearest before the eyes of men, that so thou mayest study both to please God worthily, and to edify thy fellow-men by thy life and conversation: ever remembering that whether thou dost good or evil, both are done in the sight of Him who will render to every one according to his works.

When therefore thou wilt eat or drink, when thou wilt sleep or take repose, when thou wilt follow the bent of thy desires, thou dost the works of the flesh, and thy conduct is like that of the beasts of the earth; that wander about, that eat, drink, and fill their belly, till they are satisfied; that butt with their horns, that tear with their claws or teeth, that scowl with threatening looks on those who resist them, and fill the air with hideous cries,—such are carnal men,—such the glutton—the miser—the proud—the passionate and the brawler;—for the spirit of God is not in them, and they are subject to their passions only.

3. But when thou dost watch or pray, when thou wilt read or sing psalms and hymns to the glory of God and His saints, when thou wilt fast, and abstain from vice, and make thyself useful to thy neighbour, when thou wilt mourn and weep over thy own disorders, or confess them, and supplicate pardon of God; then thou dost the works of the Holy Spirit, follow His inspirations, and fulfil the duties of a religious life. Such con-

duct is like that of the angels in heaven, who ever sing the praise and glory of God, from whose face they never turn away.

But when thou wilt give way to sentiments of anger, when thou wilt nourish pride, when thou wilt give loose to detraction and murmuring, when thou wilt commit a fraud or practice lying, when thou wilt disturb others or rejoice over the evil that has happened to thy neighbour, when his prosperity afflicts thee, when thou despisest him in thy heart, or when thou labourest diligently for thy own interest only; then thou followest the suggestions of the devil, and thy conduct, full of malice and teeming with disorder, resembles his: for that spirit of iniquity owns no counsellor but his passions,— no motive but his perverseness. He does all the evil he can, or dare; and because there is no good in him, he strives hard to seduce and pervert the sons of men.

The life of the just is like that of the angels, and the life of the carnal man like that of the beasts; but the life of the proud is like that of devils.

Servants of God, take heed, lest you fall into the snares which the spirits of malice lay for you; for you will be accused by them at the awful tribunal of God, and there confounded.

CHAP. II.

OF THE PRAISE OF GOD DURING THE BARRENNESS OR TEPIDITY OF DEVOTION.

" *Pauper et inops laudabunt nomen tuum, Domine.*"*

" *The poor and needy shall praise thy name, O Lord !*"

1. If in prayer or holy meditation, thou shouldst fall into a state of dryness, coldness or sadness, be sure not to give way to despair, or cease to call humbly on the name of Jesus.

But in poverty of spirit, persevere in giving praise and thanksgiving to God; and take comfort abundantly when reading these

* Ps. lxxiii. 21.

words: "The poor and needy shall praise thy name, O Lord!"

For, many holy and devout souls have been proved by dryness, and seemed for a long while as it were abandoned by God, that they might thereby learn patience and compassion for others, by the sense of their own sorrow and need; and not to presume too much on themselves in the moment of fervour, and in the season of spiritual jubilation.

Say with the Psalmist, "I am needy and poor."* In the Lord will I put my trust, for He is my strength and my salvation, and all good comes from God.

2. Restrain thyself then from presumption, when gladness is vouchsafed, and beware of discouragement, when the clouds of sorrow gather around: receive each

---

* Ps. xix. 6.

of these as it shall please God to send them, and in all be content; for thou hast nothing of good in thyself: all is from God.

When the grace of devotion is granted, the sun of justice shines on thee from the heights of heaven; thy soul walks in brightness and rejoices in its riches. But, if, permitting thyself to be deceived by any feeling of vanity or presumption, thou wilt confide on thy own strength, thou wilt indeed be wretched.

When the grace of devotion is withdrawn on account perhaps of the abuse made of it, thy soul becomes really poor and weak, capable of but very little, and with no relish for prayer: receive these privations with gratitude, for in withdrawing these gifts, and humbling thee with His elect, God giveth a new proof of His love.

His hand strikes thee with the rod, with which He corrects His children, for the hidden excesses and numberless acts of negligence of which thou art daily guilty, in order to inspire thee with a contempt for thyself, and to hinder thee from having so high an estimate of thy own merit; as St. Paul says, "Be not high-minded but fear."*

The soul is a great gainer when deeply penetrated with a sense of self-contempt, it gives entirely to God all the glory of the good it may have done.

* Rom. xi. 20.

CHAP. III.

ON THE PROBATION OF THE JUST BY ADVERSITY.

"*Exultate justi, in Domino.*"*

"*Rejoice in the Lord, O ye just.*"

1. Joy is eternal in heaven; sorrow is eternal in hell: both dwell occasionally on earth, to prove the good and the bad.

The sky is pure and serene in summer, dark and cloudy in winter; so also is it with the devout soul:—when the grace of God comes and illuminates it, it discovers many truths which were before unknown, and understands what before it understood not. It rejoices with great joy, and expresses in songs of gladness, the

* Ps. xxxii. 3.

happiness which it feels. But the season of trial comes at last, and the grace of devotion is withdrawn; then winter comes, in ice and cold, in the gloom of the intellect and fear of soul. Then patience, most needful to our wants as it is pleasing to God, comes to our aid; in such trials our advance in virtue grows apace, and by patience, will our eternal recompense hereafter be increased.

2. The chastisements of God humble and purify the soul, confound our pride, and dissipate all vain-glory.

So long as the soul is united to the body, so long does God prove man, in turn, under both relations, that he may make greater progress in the love of Christ.

Wherefore it is a proof of great knowledge and virtue, to profit by adversity as well as prosperity.

Bless then, O my soul, bless the Lord, at all times. Sing, O Sion, day and night, the praises of the Lord, and thy reward shall be great in the sight of God, in heaven and on earth; for all shall tend to thy spiritual advantage, whether prosperity or adversity, good or evil, joy or sorrow. Whence the apostle saith; " We know that to them that love God, all things work together unto good ;"* and nothing shall ever be wanted to those that fear Him. Blessed are they who in all things follow the will of God.

* Rom. viii. 28.

CHAP. IV.

OF THE TRUE LOVER OF GOD.

"*Diligite Dominum, omnes sancti ejus.*"*

" O Love the Lord, all ye his saints."

1. Love Him, rich and poor, love Him great and small; for it is He who made both poor and rich, both small and great.

He that would truly love God, must love Him purely; that is to say, must love God for God, and with none other wish but that of enjoying Him alone. Such love must have for its end neither temporal advantage nor profit, nor inward consolation—no—not even eternal recompense; but wholly

* Ps. xxx. 24.

and entirely for His infinite goodness and surpassing worth.

It is for this reason that the Psalmist, inviting us to sing the praises of God, says and repeats so often, " Give glory to the Lord, for He is good :"*—words which are indeed sweet to such as love God; —but, for the consolation of the contrite and repentant mourner, he adds—" For His mercy endureth for ever."

Ye weak and frail, taste ye the sweetness of these words ;—whatever be your sins, despair not— " for His mercy endureth for ever."

2. The deeper our humility, and the more fervent our love, the more pleasing shall we be to God.

Blessed is he that accounteth himself the vilest of creatures, and who shuns every thing contrary to the will of God.

* Ps. cv.

Blessed is he, who out of charity and with a pure intention, does every action for God, and with a view to please Him; and who proposes to himself no other end, than His honour, praise, and glory.

Blessed is he who attributes nothing that he possesses to his own merits, but freely returns to God all that he has received from Him.

CHAP. V.

ON THE GRATITUDE OF THE SOUL FOR EVERY GOOD.

"*Magnificate Dominum mecum, et exaltemus nomen ejus in idipsum.*"*

"*O magnify the Lord with me; and let us extol his name together.*"

1. He that for the least favour, is most grateful to God, gives Him worthy praise, and appreciates the goodness and bounty of Him, who above all is infinitely great; for no grace can be small or contemptible, that comes from the liberal hand of the Most High.

God seeks and asks for nothing, but that our love may be disinterested; and that by carefully avoiding all offence against him, we

* Ps. xxxiii.

should everywhere and always give proofs to Him of our sincere gratitude.

2. Great in the sight of God is he, who is filled with deep humility, and contempt for himself—who judges himself unworthy to partake in His gifts and benefits, and when he makes use of such as he has received, seeks neither to satiate his vanity, nor to court the esteem of men.

But greater is he, who although like Job, afflicted, overwhelmed with contempt and injuries, despoiled of his goods, abandoned by his friends, tempted by the devil, loaded with derision, and covered with confusion,—yet rejoices in tribulation, giving thanks to God, and blessing His holy name; reckons as great gain to his soul, the evils and calamities, which weigh heavy upon him; and endures them all without murmur, for the love of God.

3. Blessed is he, who after the example of Job, learns to acknowledge the hand which strikes him, and to submit with pious resignation to the rod of affliction; trusting wholly to the mercy of God, and bowing unreservedly to His holy will.

Blessed is he who ever seeks after, and prefers before all, the will of God, and who takes pleasure in being accounted vile in the eyes of man:—who rejoices in the midst of insult and injury, and who receives temporal losses as ministering servants to the good of his soul

CHAP. VI.

ON THE CONFORMITY OF THE DEVOUT SOUL TO THE CROSS.

"*Cum ipso sum in tribulatione.*"*

"*I am with him in tribulation.*"

1. *The faithful Soul.*—Lord, what mean those words that I hear? "Give to thy servant a right understanding;"—unfold to me all the consolation these words inclose.

The Lord.—Hearken unto Me, my son.

When thy heart is fallen into tribulation or anguish of soul, then art thou fastened with Jesus to His cross.

When consolations return in the fervour of devotion, and thou art constrained to express thy joy,

* Ps. xc. 15.

by the singing of hymns and holy canticles, then art thou raised again with Jesus, in newness of spirit; then dost thou rise again from the dead, singing alleluias of joy.

2. When on bended knees, thou implorest pardon of thy sins, lamenting and deploring them in the bottom of thy heart; then with repeated blows, thou knockest loudly at the gate of heaven.

When turning away from the vanities of the world, thou givest thyself up entirely to the meditation of the good things of eternity; then thou mountest to heaven with Jesus, to live there in the company of the angels.

Be then meek, humble, and resigned to the infirmities and reverses which may come upon thee in the service of God; patiently bear thy cross with Jesus; die daily on the cross, for thy eternal salvation; for every affliction of the flesh, when borne with patience, is a remedy for the evils of the soul, a satisfaction for sins, and the hope of future blessedness and glory. Amen.

CHAP. VII.

ON THE WALKING OF A PURE SOUL WITH GOD.

" Ambulate, dum lucem habetis."*

" Walk whilst you have the light."

1. He walketh with God, whilst there is light, who has no desire for what this world affords; and who fixes all his affections on God in heaven: for the hidden treasure of the faithful soul is Jesus Christ

---

* Joan. xii. 35.

our Lord, in whom all goodness dwells.

He is always in indigence and want, however great his riches, who has not God for his friend: but he that would have God for his friend must love Him, and keep His commandments.

2. He keeps the commandments of God who avoids all idle and useless words; who shows by his works, an example of those virtues he recommends in practice; when, instead of seeking his own glory, he refers all the glory and the good he may do, or observe in others, purely and entirely to the glory of God.

But he that is satisfied with himself, pleases a fool, and displeases God.

Thus in all the good thou sayest or dost, seek only the glory of God, that thou mayest receive from Him still greater favours.

Why shouldst thou glory in natural advantages, whereas thou art a mere mortal and must shortly become the food of worms?

Young man, hear the voice of an ancient; separate thyself from all that might allure thy soul to idleness and distraction; for thou shalt find repose only by descending into thy heart, and disposing it to seek God before all things, and to love Him intimately.

CHAP. VIII.

ON THE PEACE OF HEART, AND REST IN GOD.

"*In pace factus est locus ejus.*"*

"*His place is in peace.*"

1 *The faithful Soul.*—Lord, who is he that dwelleth in true peace?

The Lord.—He that is meek, and humble of heart. But why dost thou seek to inquire into the state of others, while thou neglectest thyself in many things?

Hearken then unto me; it is the heart the most humble, and the most willing to suffer for the sake of God, that enjoys the most abundant peace.

To such a one no burthen is

* Ps. lxxv. 3.

heavy, for he hath God himself in his heart.

Blessed are they that converse with God in prayer,—in meditation,—by sacred songs,—by reading; and who keep silence on the vanities of the passing world.

Wherever thou art, wheresoever thou goest, whithersoever thou fliest, thy thoughts still accompany thee; but pious meditation brings joy to the soul, while evil thoughts afflict it.

Anger brings forth trouble, and envy blinds the soul; but hatred kills it.

Devout reading instructs; prayer enflames; but good works are the fulfilment of the law.

2. Holy words purify the heart; frivolous words defile it; idle words scandalize it; bitter words sadden it; words of mercy soothe disquietude; moral conversation edi-

fies the heart; learned or dogmatic entertainments strengthen the faith, and heavenly words elevate it to the throne of the Divinity.

Cleanse then thy heart from all malice, if thou wouldst enjoy sweet peace.

There is no sweet peace but what comes from God, and dwells in the virtuous soul, which performs all things well for the sake of God, whom it loves.

Abide in silence, and endure a little for the sake of God; and He himself will free thee from every burthen, and from all disquietude.

A holy life and a pure conscience beget confidence in God in tribulation and death; but an evil conscience is always in fear, always at war,—tormented by remorse.

The angry man falls quickly from one evil into a worse; but the patient and the meek makes a friend of his enemy, and God will be propitious to him, for that he hath shewn mercy unto him who offended him.

CHAP. IX.

ON RECOLLECTION OF THE HEART WITH GOD.

" *Quis non colligit mecum, spargit.*"*

" *He who gathereth not with me, scattereth,*"—*saith our Lord Jesus Christ.*

1. When through the multiplied temptations of the evil one, the bitter passions of thy own heart, or annoyances from thy fellow-men, thou shalt have fallen into luke-

* Matt. xii. 30.

warmness, dissipation or distraction of mind, retire into solitude, and there prostrate and alone at the foot of the Holy Cross, or before the image of the blessed Virgin Mary or any other picture consecrated either to the honour of God, or the memory of His saints, use thy endeavour to calm and gather up thy soul by reciting the Lord's Prayer, and the Angelical Salutation.

Invoke especially Jesus and Mary, beseech the holy angels, and all the heavenly court, to obtain a return of the graces and consolations of which thou hast been deprived, and say with holy David, " Lord, all my desire is before Thee, and my groaning is not hidden from thee."* Lord, from my youth I have put my hope in Thee; unto Thee I fly in my tribulation.

* Ps. xxxvii. 10.

A DEVOUT PRAYER.

Teach me, O Lord, ever to follow Thy commandments, to do Thy will, and to renounce my own; for this is well-pleasing to Thee and indispensably necessary to the safety of my soul.

O Lord, may I never think, nor desire, nor do any thing displeasing to Thee, or injurious to my neighbour:—never act contrary to what Thou hast commanded me, or Thy devout and faithful servants.

If I transgress, correct me in Thy mercy, and destroy me not in Thy wrath.

Because thou art my God, and I am Thy servant—ever poor—ever weak, and ever most needy of Thy grace and mercy in all things.

Blessed be Thy holy name above all, now and for ever more! Amen.

CHAP. X.

ON WATCHING AND PRAYER AGAINST TEMPTATIONS.

" *Vigilate et orate ut non intretis in tentationem.*"*

" *Watch and pray that you enter not into temptation,*"—either of the flesh, or the spirit, of the world or the devil.

1. The flesh excites us to concupiscence, the spirit to pride, the world to vanity, the devil to envy: but Christ hath taught us quite the contrary. He exhorts us to practice chastity, humility, charity, and contempt for the world; if we would avoid the pains of hell and deserve the kingdom of heaven.

To this end we must watch and

* Mar<. xiv. 38.

pray, at all times and in every place; for no part is secure against the attacks of our malignant enemy who sleeps not, nor rests from his temptations, " who continually goes about seeking whom he may devour,"*—whom he may cast into trouble and discouragement, and whom he may inspire with disgust for prayer, or other spiritual exercises.

2. It is for this reason that our Lord Jesus Christ, knowing the malice of the evil one, the efficacy of prayer, the strength of the enemy, and the weakness of man, admonishes, in the most earnest manner, His disciples, and all the faithful, to watch and pray, if they would not be overcome by their enemies,—that is, their vices.

Watch ye then and pray, that ye enter not into the temptations

* 1 Pet. v. 8.

of the devil, nor consent unto him.

If thou art unable to recite the whole psalter or other long prayers, recite a psalm, a verse, a devout hymn in honour of Jesus, of Mary, or of some of the blessed saints, that thou mayest raise up thy soul to God, by the groanings of thy heart or the holy words thy mouth may utter.

For God is nigh unto all them that call upon Him with humility; and " the prayer of him that humbleth himself shall pierce the clouds,"*—shall fill the soul with trust in God, and thwart the schemes, the efforts, the threats, and the vanities of the devil.

3. If the presence of men keep thee from prayer, " Enter," according to the counsel of Jesus Christ, " into thy chamber, and having

* Eccles. xxxv. 21.

shut the door, pray to thy Father in secret,"* who already knoweth the thoughts and desires of thy heart, and of what thou hast need.

Say unto Him, then, every time thou wilt address Him in prayer,—" Father! Thy will be ever done, and not mine; grant me nothing but what may be conformable to Thy glory, and the good of my soul."

When thou art in choir with thy brethren, or in church with the faithful, read and sing with a recollection like that of the angels before the throne of God.

Sing in such a manner that thy heart may be inwardly penetrated with compunction, and that thou mayest please men without displeasing God and His holy angels; for God prefers compunction of heart, to a loud or tuneful voice.

* Matt. vi. 6.

God is appeased by humble prayer, but offended by vain glory.

The groanings of a contrite heart draw down the grace of God, and impart strength to virtue; but the song of a wandering heart quenches devotion: for all such faults and negligences we must give a strict account.

May the divine mercy keep us from all such offences, and lead us to the kingdom of heaven! Amen.

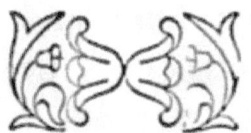

CHAP. XI.

ON THE FEAR OF ETERNAL PUNISHMENT, AS A PRESERVATIVE AGAINST THE VICES OF THE FLESH AND PRIDE OF SPIRIT.

"*Confige timore tuo carnes meas.*"*

"*Pierce thou my flesh with thy fear.*"

1. Such a prayer is good to repress the evil inclinations of the flesh, and humble the pride of the spirit; because these two enemies fight against man and harass him daily: for either the flesh torments him by its irregular appetites, or the spirit seeks the praise of men:—applying its own good works to the gratification of vanity.

* Ps. cxviii. 120.

Both of these enemies are great evils, and from either side there is imminent peril.

When thou art drawn to evil, by that miserable flesh, so shortly doomed to be the prey of death, think of the torments of eternal fire. Thus shalt thou extinguish the fires of concupiscence, by thinking on those of hell : for it is happily ordered that impressions more feeble should disappear before those which are stronger, that the soul may be saved " so as by fire."*

Short is the duration of all carnal pleasure:—beauty of body, glory, honours,—all the enjoyments of this world, are vain and deceitful.

As a violent headache forces complaints and groans, even from the thoughtless and the negligent, so the fear of death, and the dread of the punishment of hell, cause

* 1 Cor. iii. 15.

the man subject to his passions, to resist temptation, and abstain from sin.

2. He that is without fear, shall quickly fall into evil: and he that refuses to humble himself, in the presence of God and His saints, shall be confounded by devils in the day of judgment, and cruelly tormented by them for ever.

Listen to an irrevocable decree, applicable to every creature,—to angels as well as to men:—" God resisteth the proud, and giveth grace to the humble."*

But the mercy of the Lord is with His saints and elect, from eternity unto eternity.

Tremble, then, proud man, at the judgment of God in all thy actions, and cease to glory in the vanity of a passing reputation.

When thou hast done all that

* Jas. iv. 6.

thou canst, and all that thou oughtst to have done, there yet remain many things, and scarcely couldst thou restore one for a thousand.

Tremble then at the rod and staff of God's vengeance—tremble on account of the judgment to come.

Every virtue shall be rewarded, but every bad action shall be punished.

If fire were to break out in thy dwelling, wouldst thou not fear?—wouldst thou not rise on the instant and fly? Such is the effect that ought to be produced in thy soul by the fear, and dread and thoughts of the pains to come, which shall never end; and whoever entertains in his heart a lively horror—a salutary dread—of the punishments of hell, shall thereby overcome lukewarmness, and rekindle his fervour.

CHAP. XII.

ON THE MEMORY OF OUR LORD'S PASSION, AS A REMEDY AGAINST DISSIPATION OR DISTRACTION OF MIND.

" *Beati qui lugent, quoniam ipsi consolabuntur.*"*

" *Blessed are those who weep, for they shall be comforted.*"

1. By whom shall they be comforted? most surely by Christ—in the secret of the heart, and not by the world with its vain consolations and idle frivolities.

Light and trifling discourses, pleasant jests, and frequent laughter, have no agreement with the sacred passion and bitter sufferings of Christ

* Matt. v. 3.

Were my head or my back wounded, even by one of those sharp thorns which formed the crown of Jesus Christ, would I laugh and be merry? no, surely, but rather weep and cry aloud through pain.

Were my foot pierced by one of the nails which fastened Jesus to the cross, whither could I go, or whither could I run? Doubtless I could neither go nor run anywhere: I would lay me down in sorrow, and learn by the experience of pain, to mourn over the sufferings of my divine Saviour.

Happy should I be, if the abundance and bitterness of my tears could then efface my sins.

Oh! how holy is the grief we feel, and how sweet the tears we shed, when we weep over the sacred wounds of our Saviour Jesus Christ!

2. Whenever, then, thou art in distress, or assailed by any temptation, or on the point of yielding to some concealed weakness, arm thyself forthwith with the shield of prayer, and the standard of the Holy Cross; take refuge in the sacred wounds of Christ, and there in the fervour of prayer, and in serious meditation on His passion, find a salutary remedy for all the wants of thy soul.

Consider well the ponderous, high, and heavy cross, on which Jesus Christ hung naked;—fastened and transpierced with nails for the love of thee.

Behold his crown;—count there the numerous thorns, which pierced so sadly his sacred head, and bedewed it abundantly with his sacred blood.

Place these, as well as the other instruments used in the passion of

Jesus Christ, beside thee as a safeguard by day and night: lest thy malignant enemy, the devil, finding thy mind stripped of these sacred representations, enter in and pollute thy heart with vain thoughts and dangerous suggestions.

3. Let not therefore thy bed be aid in softness:—in memory of he holy nativity of our Lord Jesus Christ, think of that crib, poor and narrow but replete with all virtues, where Jesus was born, and where were heard His infant cries. He had no ornament for His cradle but a little straw, and no nourishment but a little milk from His Virgin Mother.

Let the hardness and poverty of thy couch, recal in some sort, the hard and stony sepulchre of our Lord Jesus Christ; crucified for thy sake, truly dead and buried in the bosom of the earth, and covered with a great stone.

There then, seek repose, in the peace of the Lord, forgetting the world and all its vanities; despising all that is reckoned great and pleasing in the eyes of men; that rising with Him from thy slumber thou mayest come forth refreshed in virtue and grace, and at the last day be raised again to share in the eternal glory of the elect. Amen.

CHAP. XIII

ON THE INVOCATION OF THE HOLY NAME OF JESUS, AND OF THE BLESSED MARY, HIS VIRGIN MOTHER.

"*Dirige, Domine, Deus meus, in conspectu tuo viam meam.*"*

"O Lord, my God, direct my way in thy sight."

1. Thy ways, O Lord Jesus Christ, are beautiful and pure; and to those that walk therein, thy paths are safe, and right, and perfect.

All thy paths are peaceful and holy, and lead the faithful and humble of heart, to the kingdom of heaven.

Wherever thou mayest go, or

* Ps. v. 9.

mayest direct thy steps, wherever thou shalt rest or sojourn, call upon Jesus, call upon Mary, His holy Mother: with confidence repeat these words of the psalmist, as the guide of thy way; "Direct, O Lord, my way in thy sight:" then add the following,—"Perfect thou my goings," O Jesus, "in Thy paths, that my footsteps be not moved," to behold vanity, or to wound my soul, by words of idleness.

2. Next let this comfortable prayer be for thy life's viaticum,— a provision for thy journey;—let it be as a staff for thy firm support;— say it often, say it devoutly:—

"*Jesus and Mary, be ever with me in the way, as my good guards at all times and in every place, lest I wander in bye-paths; lest my senses or my heart be seduced by the many illusions within and without.*"

This holy prayer, "Jesus and Mary," is short, easily remembered, and carried about without inconvenience; it is sweet and pleasing to the mind; the poor pilgrim who flies from the vanities of the world, will find in it the consolation, strength, and protection which he is in need of, to hold on his course in safety; it will refresh the fatigue of the journey, and calm the disquietude of his soul; it will fill him with comfort, and aid him mightily in resisting the obstacles which he may meet with; and it will help to lead him by a path direct to life eternal.

This holy prayer is addressed to surer companions, and a more powerful escort, than all the kings and princes of this world, and to higher saints than all the saints in heaven or on earth.

This prayer spoken fervently

will aid in procuring the favour of all the court of heaven; who with all reverence, ever follow Jesus Christ their Lord, and Mary, their holy lady, the blessed mother of Jesus, most worthy of all praise, and of the homage and benediction of all created things.

He that has these for his companions in his earthly pilgrimage, shall find in them devoted and zealous patrons in the hour of death.

Never depart from Jesus and Mary on earth, if thou wouldst live and rejoice with Jesus and Mary for ever in heaven.

Thy steps will be more secure, with less fear of wandering, if thou hast Jesus and Mary in thy heart; if they be the object of thy praise, thy benediction, thy applause, thy transports, thy cries of delight, the joy of thy heart, thy tears and sighs, thy aim, thy embraces, thy regards, and thy adoration.

3. Blessed are those who call on Jesus and Mary continually,—who salute them devoutly,—who recall them lovingly to their memory,—who honour them above all,—who sing their praise with lively joy,—who glorify them to the utmost height,—who love them ardently,—who make their love the delight of their souls,—and who deem it happiness to sing and celebrate their names for ever.

Oh, how sweet is Jesus! how sweet is holy Mary, his beloved mother!

Blessed is the pilgrim, who in the time of his exile, is ever mindful of the celestial country; where Jesus and Mary are surrounded by angels and saints in joy ineffable and glory without end.

Blessed is the pilgrim who seeks

no dwelling-place on earth, who desires "to be dissolved and to be with Christ in heaven."

Blessed is the poor and needy, who every day beggeth the bread of heaven, and who ceases not to stretch forth his suppliant hands, till he receives the crumbs which fall from the table of his Lord.

Blessed is he that is invited to the Supper of the Lamb, who here below receives the sacrament of His love and waits in patience until called to sit down to the banquet in heaven.

4. Because, as often as a person receives the communion devoutly, or as often as the priest reverently and devoutly offers to the honour of God the holy sacrifice; so often does he sit at the table with Jesus, and His blessed Mother, to eat and drink spiritually with them.

Such a one is the disciple of Jesus, the minister of the blessed Virgin Mary, the companion of the angels, the fellow-citizen of the Apostles, the servant of God, is nearly allied to the saints, and the intimate friend of Heaven.

He flies the tumult of the world; he turns away from idle talk; he meditates on the words of Jesus, and watches carefully over his heart and affections, that no thought may enter there to offend Jesus, or Mary, or the saints.

"He shall receive a blessing from the Lord, and mercy from God his Saviour."* Whensoever he shall call upon Him, He shall hear him from His holy heaven—wheresoever he may be, and whatsoever danger may oppress him.

For the disciples were on the sea, in danger of sinking, and they

* Ps. xxiii. 5

called on Jesus, and Jesus appeared forthwith, and said to them. " Why are ye fearful ?"* " Be of good heart, it is I. fear ye not."†

The voice of Jesus is a voice full of sweetness to bring consolation ; of power to protect ; of joy to make the soul glad ; of indulgence to pardon, and of grace to lead to life eternal.

* John vi. 20. † Matt. xiv. 27.

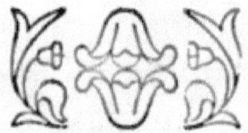

CHAP. XIV.

ON THE NECESSITY OF STRUGGLING MANFULLY AGAINST VICE, AFTER THE EXAMPLE OF THE SAINTS.

"*Viriliter agite, et confortetur cor vestrum.*"*

" Do ye *manfully*, and let your heart be strengthened."

1. As the passion and cross of Jesus, and the sufferings of the martyrs, teach us to bear the pains and crosses of this life; so the purity of the blessed Virgin Mary, the chastity of the holy virgins, widows and saints of God, show how we may overcome temptations of the flesh, despise the riches, fly the honours, and renounce all the vanities of the world, to give our-

* Ps. xxx. 25.

selves up entirely to the love and pursuit of heavenly things.

O servant of God, walk in the foot-steps of those courageous souls, who have given thee the example of invincible patience:—like them, resist the devil and all his temptations.

Consider the unshaken constancy of weak and delicate virgins, and learn from them to despise and cast from thee with contempt, all sensual pleasures, and every other vice.

If God in His mercy has granted thee temporal riches,—thou, who art nothing,—use not these to satiate vanity,—fix not on them thy foolish heart; for thou knowest not how soon thou mayest be taken away from them, nor how long thou mayest enjoy them.

Ask not long life;—seek rather for a good and pious one;—for the witness of a good conscience is better than all the treasures of this world:—because the greater thy riches on earth, the more rigorous the account to be rendered in heaven.

2. Ah! how deceitful is the favour of this world! how short its glory! for after the enjoyment of its riches, its honours, its dignities, and its delights, come the tears and groans, and dreadful punishments of hell, whence, alas! there is no redemption.

But oh! how great is the happiness of the elect! they are with God, with His angels and saints; inebriated with a happiness which comprehends all joys and shall never end.

Happy men and wise virgins! oh! how happy ye!—who have renounced all for the love of Christ, anxiously endeavouring to walk in the narrow path that leads to the eternal kingdom.

3. Learn then, faithful and devout servants of Jesus Christ, that during this life, ye must watch, and pray, and fast, and labour, and fight against the divers temptations of the flesh and the spirit.

The flesh must be mortified, lest it rise and lust against the spirit;—lest it seduce the soul and prevailing over it, draw it down to hell.

To what purpose is the body pampered delicately in this world, if when it quits this passing life, it must endure hell's fearful torments.

And what boots it to be praised and honoured by men here on earth, and so soon afterwards to be humbled and condemned to dwell eternally with the spirit of darkness, and the impious sons of the evil one?

To enjoy the reputation of a

great and learned man in this world, and not be counted in the number of the elect, is a subject of shame and confusion in the eyes of God and His saints: but to suffer for Christ, and to be despised by the wicked for His sake, is high honour, praise, and glory supreme with God and all His saints.

Hence the words of consolation which Jesus Christ addresses to His disciples, and to all who suffer injury or distress for His sake :— " Blessed are ye when they shall revile you, and persecute you, and speak all that is evil against you for My sake ; be glad and rejoice, for your reward is very great in heaven."*

* Matt. v. 11-12

CHAP. XV.

ON THE LOVE OF RETIREMENT AND HOLY PERSEVERANCE.

"*Stabiles estote—in opere Domini semper.*"*

"*Be ye steadfast—in the work of the Lord always.*"

1. Answer me, my dear brother, what advantage, dost thou find towards thy sanctification by hurrying hither and thither,—by hearing and seeing many and various things, which of a certainty, tend to exclude from the kingdom of heaven?

Blessed is he that lives in retirement and recollection, who enters into himself, who keeps a strict watch over his heart and body, and who asks pardon of God with sighs

* 1 Cor. xv. 58.

and tears for his frequent distractions.

Woe to you, who so often and so heedlessly mix in the vain bustle of the world, who shun solitude, who waste unprofitably a portion of your precious time, and who thereby cause scandal to others.

Inward peace is laid up abundantly for him who loveth solitude;—who gives his heart in secret to God,—who prays frequently,—who is employed in useful occupations,—who feeds his soul with Sacred Scriptures and other holy studies, and meditates with ardent affection, on the truths of salvation.

2. The idler and the babbler deserve severe reproof, and their fellowship must be shunned, lest they corrupt the simple by the frivolity of their discourse; or, by the ir-

regularity of their manners, bring trouble and scandal into the souls of the little ones.

Oh! brother, oh! thou whose heart is dissipated and fond of idle jests, dread the pains of purgatory; where, for every act of trifling, every idle word or evil thought, thou must be punished by bitter stripes from infernal tormentors.

It is much better then to live here in fear and trembling, in penance and tears than to share the lot of the reprobate hereafter, and to be tormented together with them, by devils for all eternity.

There is surely no joy nor mirth in the fire of hell, whence none can ever draw thee out.

3. He that would reflect often on these truths, and seriously meditate thereon, would soon conceive a disgust for all worldly vanities, and abhor all sensual desires; that so

he might avoid eternal punishment, and after death obtain eternal happiness.

But woe unto those on earth, and heavier woe to come, on those who are but lightly moved by the thought of the divine judgments, and by the fear of sufferings which their body has not yet experienced.

CHAP. XVI.

ON DIVINE CONSOLATION IN TRIBULATION FOR CHRIST'S SAKE.

"*In mundo pressuram habebitis; sed confidite. Ego vici mundum.*"*

"*In the world you shall have distress; but have confidence, I have overcome the world.*"

1. "It is a comfort to have a companion in misery," saith the pro-

* Joan. xvi. 33.

verb. But who is that friend so affectionate and so good, who shares our miseries and sympathizes in our infirmities? That friend is Jesus Christ our Lord, who suffered and was crucified for us; and who, in the gospel, calls Himself the physician and shepherd of our souls, the comforter of the poor, the weak and the afflicted; the physician of the sick, and the stay of those that fall:—for "they that are well," says He, "have no need of a physician, but they that are sick."* And in like manner David speaks of Him, when he addresses these words of comfort to afflicted souls, "the Lord is nigh unto them that are of a contrite heart;"† and in another Psalm, to give confidence to his servant, proved by temptations and tribulations, God himself says,

* Mark ii. 17. † Ps. xxxiii. 19.

"I am with him in tribulation, I will deliver him, and I will glorify him."*

Truly there is much comfort and consolation to all that are sad or afflicted with many calamities; whereas Christ was Himself tempted and afflicted, and stricken with many sorrows, for our sake.

2. God, who is sovereignly good and just in all His ways, would not send pains and tribulations in this life if they were not useful and salutary to our souls.

And who art thou, sinner, who art thou, loaded with many sins?—who art thou who wilt dare, in affliction, to wince under the hand of Him who spared not His own Son?—for it is meet and just that the guilty and unprofitable servant should bear without murmuring the light corrections which his master

* Ps. xc. 15.

inflicts on him; since His well-beloved Son,—and He all innocence, was wounded with so many stripes.

It is meet and just that a sick man, anxious to recover his health, should sip some drops from the bitter chalice, which already his physician—who required no such remedy—had drained before him, to neutralize the mortal poison, with which, humanity had been so deeply infected, and to cure perfectly and free from eternal death, erring man, whom sin had deprived of life spiritual, as well as corporal.

The heavy burthen of the servant should be much alleviated by the remembrance of the heavier burthen of sorrows that his innocent master has borne; and the sick should be much comforted in his sufferings, when he reflects that these, if borne with resignation, shall serve to cleanse him from sins, and to assure his hope of life eternal.

3. It is, indeed, great and glorious for a poor slave to be clothed with the same cloth as his master; and to wear, as son and heir, the royal purple, that will give a title to assist at the eternal spousals of the Lamb.

The cloth with which Jesus is clothed, is humility of heart, self-denial, the privation of necessary things, patience in adversity, and perseverance in virtue.

He that receives with gratitude the chastisements which God inflicts on him, finds in his sorrows, the safety of his soul, and shall receive in heaven a fairer crown of glory.

"Blessed is he that understandeth, concerning the needy and the poor,"* Jesus, who though richer

* Ps. xl. 1-2.

than all, willed, for the love of us, to become needy and poor. Blessed is he, that despising the riches and ease of this life, walks wisely in His footsteps, and takes up His cross daily to the hour of his death for the safety of his soul.

CHAP. XVII.

ON WATCHING OVER THE CONSCIENCE, IN EVERY PLACE AND AT ALL TIMES.

"*Anima mea in manibus meis semper.*"*

"*My soul is continually in my hands.*"

1. Nothing is more useful or more salutary for one desirous of attain-

* Ps. cxviii. 109.

ing eternal life, than to meditate continually on the salvation of his soul.

Open every book of piety—run through all the treatises on the spiritual life, the soul will find no salvation but in God, and in a virtuous life.

Hence the Lord and Redeemer of souls said to His disciples, "What doth it profit a man, if he gain the whole world and suffer the loss of his own soul?"*

He that meditates often on these words, and who is more seriously concerned for the welfare of his soul than for the increase of his fortune, or for the entertainment of his body, is a merchant truly wise;† for he prefers spiritual riches, which perish not, to the perishable goods of earth.

He is one of those good and

* Matt. xvi. 26. † Matt. xiii. 45.

faithful servants of Christ, who makes his two talents four, his five ten: and who on receiving only one, instead of hiding it in the earth, laying it apart, throwing it away, or treating it with contempt, distributes it to the poor, that he may have part in their prayers; or offers it at the altar of God, returning thanks to the Lord, for the smallest benefits received.*

Blessed is the good servant who is faithful in a little,† who employs every moment of his life in a useful manner; who is not busied in what concerns him not, and who, to please God, becomes like one that is deaf and dumb. He walks in peace through the tumult of the world, "having his soul continually in his hands."

Take no thought then of the conduct of thy neighbour, but in as far

* Matt. xxv. 14, 15, *et infra*. † Luke xix. 17.

as the love of God and charity may require.

2. Covet not the praises of men, for they are vain. Be not afraid of their reproach; for, far from hurting thy soul, humiliations purify, and make it worthy to receive in heaven a more brilliant crown ; and none deserve to be glorified in the kingdom of heaven who cannot endure reproach for the love of God on earth.

A MEDITATION AND PRAYER.

Since then thou hast suffered for the love of me, O my God, it is but fitting that I should suffer for the love of Thee ; and that I should walk in Thy footsteps as far as I am able.

Thou hast said to St. Peter, " Follow thou Me,"* but alas ! how little can I bear for Thee !

* John. xxi. 22.

I make many resolutions, but scarcely one in ten, do I execute: my words are many, but my works are few; all blame is mine; there is no excuse; idleness and indifference increase each day the number of my sins. What should I think or say on these offences? alas! nought remains but to entreat thy mercy, and to cry, " Lord, I have sinned, have mercy upon me."

Thus were led all the saints that have gone before us; such are the lessons they have left us; such, each day, is still the conduct of all thy faithful.

Oh all ye saints and friends of God, pray for me; for I am weak and indigent, and I humbly implore the assistance of all.

THE PRAYER OF THE POOR.

O Thou Holy of holies, O Lord my God, incline Thine ear to the prayer of Thy poor servant ; " *Help me, and I shall be saved, and I will meditate always on thy justifications.*"*

Oh that I may deserve to be one of the least of Thy servants, in the kingdom which Thou hast prepared for those who are humble and who love Thee.

I will love Thee then, O Lord, my strength, with all my heart, as Thou thyself, hast commanded by Thy sacred mouth.

Thou art my hope, and my salvation, and my desire is ever towards Thee.

Keep me from all error, by a clear understanding ;—from all impurity by a clean heart ;—from all kind of doubt, by a right faith ;—from all distrust, by a steadfast hope ;—from all disgust and negligence, by an ardent charity ;—from all disquietude

* Ps. cxviii. 117.

by invincible patience;—from all unclean thoughts by holy meditation;—from the attacks of the devil, by continual prayer;—from frequent distractions, by a sustained attention in reading;—from listlessness and drowsiness, by useful occupation,—and from thinking of satisfying my vices, by the remembrance of thy holy passion. Come with all these graces, O Lord, and confirm me in all Thy holy words. Amen

CHAP. XVIII.

ON SOLITUDE AND SILENCE.

" *Ecce elongavi fugiens, et mansi in solitudine.*"*

" Lo, I have gone far off, flying away, and I abode in the wilderness."

1. And why?—because of the numerous advantages which will come to my soul in so doing; as well as to guard and restrain my heart from the various distractions with which the world allures the senses.

What the eye has not seen, or the ear has not heard, can neither excite our regret, nor trouble the peace of our soul.

Solitude and silence therefore

* Ps. liv. 8.

are profitable to inward peace, and dispose us for the gift of fervent prayer; and it is much more easy to find solitude and silence in the retirement of the closet, than in the tumult of the world.

As the fish soon dies when taken out of the water, so a pious man, who allows himself to be carried away by the world, speedily yields to distraction and becomes sullied in soul.

The wise bee abandons the flower as soon as it has gathered the honey, and returns with joy to deposit in its hive, the provisions that are to nourish it in the dearth of winter; wherefore it lays up carefully in its cell the treasure of its sweetness, before it resumes its airy course, lest it lose the fruit of its labours. For precious perfumes become more sweet by being put in a close vessel, but lose, in a little time, all their virtue when exposed to the open air.

Flowers in like manner, long preserve their beauty in the enclosure of a garden, whose walls protect them, but quickly fade when gathered by the hand of man.

Roses bloom freshly in the sheltered inclosure; but wither in the public way, and are trodden under foot.

2. So does the pious and religious man lose the sweetness of devotion, when lightness or inconstancy often leads him into the tumult of the world; but he that flies from its distraction, sheds abroad from his retreat the sweet odour of sanctity.

Exposed to the wind the taper is extinguished,—enclosed in a lanthorn it continues to burn; so is it with devotion; it is preserved most securely in the secret chamber, but is soon dissipated if exposed to the agitation of worldly business.

Love, then, solitude and silence, if thou wouldst enjoy devotion and peace of heart; for he that would move among men unhurt, must, indeed, be well covered in armour of a celestial kind,—unshaken faith, well grounded hope, and ardent charity.

Like the blessed Virgin Mary, who dwelt alone in her chamber, entertaining her soul with the holy angel, whom God had sent to her from Heaven; may the love of devotion keep thee in solitude and in thy closet, that to thee also may come the holy angel, the messenger of heaven, and faithful guardian of thy soul, and that thou mayest keep off the evil one, and all his illusions.

A devout lover of silence hath

said, "It is seldom, after much conversation with men, that my conscience has not something to reproach me with:—and another, "Our words should be very edifying, to be preferred before silence:"—and a third, "That a word is indeed good when spoken in season:"—lastly, a fourth adds, "He that keepeth his mouth closed, shall not be guilty of detraction or lying."

3. With what esteem and pleasure does not one listen to the discourse of a man who permits nothing bad, nothing vain, nothing deceitful, nothing false to pass his lips.

Many speak much, and of many things; but never without peril, for the tongue is naturally prone to evil. He that cleaves to solitude, watches over his tongue, and prays frequently, shall find much peace.

Esteem the good man who practises virtue in silence; rebuke the babbler who gives himself up to idle words; but avoid the crafty dissembler.

Fly from the tumult of the world; love a silent and retired life: imitate the humble and devout; bear patiently with those that molest thee, for the sake of Christ crucified.

4. A novice once asked an aged brother which rule or statute in the Ordinal was the most sure means of attaining true peace and devotion, the old man gave him this remarkable answer: "Keep the silence enjoined by thy fathers, avoid the tumult of men, and shun idleness."

There are three things indispensable in a religious life, and are moreover most pleasing to God and His angels:—

1st. Manual labour, to overcome sloth:—2nd. The study and reading of holy books, to prevent dis-

relish and weariness of heart:—
3rd. The continual use of prayer, to counteract the stratagems of the devil.

The ancient fathers of a spiritual life, taught, and the modern ones repeat after them, that silence and prayer draw down benedictions from God, give to the soul profound light, and dispose it to meditate with much fruit on the highest mysteries.

But he that lives in dissipation and distraction of mind, and who fosters idleness by frivolous discourse, makes himself unworthy of the heavenly gifts and becomes a trouble to his brethren.

The vain man cannot long keep silence, for he wishes to pass for wise, and to be praised above others.

He that talks presumptuously is deservedly blamed by many; but he that keeps a modest silence obtains the esteem of all.

He that despises himself, and who thinks others better than himself, shows great humility of heart; but great is the pride of him who is self-sufficient, who persists in his own opinion contrary to the will of God, and in opposition to all his brethren.

This vice is the most dangerous leprosy of all; what God abhors and often strikes with sudden death.

He that is simple and innocent, and submits humbly to authority, shall be always in joy, and nothing shall shake his security.

Be sparing in words; avoid frivolous conversation; speak nothing but what is profitable; do all things with modesty; so shall thy praise be great among thy brethren.

"Be moderate in all things—moderation is the fairest of virtues,"* and so Christ himself teaches us: "Have salt in you, and peace among you."†

And the apostle St. Paul: "Let your speech be always in grace, seasoned with salt."‡

And holy Job, when he says, "Can an unsavoury thing be eaten that is not seasoned with salt."§

5. The chaste and modest man sets a continual watch over his mouth and heart, and all his affections, that naturally incline to evil, lest he fall into sin, and offend God, or his neighbour: but there is no compunction in the heart of him who takes pleasure in listening to idle tales, and repeating them to others.

He that guards not his heart and sets not a watch at the gate of his lips, shall lose in a very little

---

* Cato. † Mark ix. 49.
‡ Coloss. iv. 6. § Job vi. 6.

while the grace of compunction; and a religious man, fond of talking, soon passes the bounds of moderate conversation.

If thou hadst the crucified Jesus in thy heart, thy mouth would not lend itself so easily to vain and idle conversation; but since thou hast not Jesus steadfast in thy heart, thou seekest abroad for consolations, weak and illusory, and but ill-adapted to calm the afflictions of that heart; for Jesus alone can afford it true consolation, and heal the wounds which sin has made.

In a little moment, with one word, He can assuage all thy infirmities; for the grace of God is more powerful for good, than the influence of the evil one is suggestive of evil.

Why dost thou lend thy ears to the vain rumours of the world; which so often trouble and distract the heart? Why dost thou refuse to listen to the sweet instructions of Christ, who day and night offers thee consolation and strength against all tribulations.

CHAP. XIX.

ON THE REFUGE OF THE POOR, IN GOD THEIR HELPER.

"*Tibi derelictus est pauper, orphano tu eris adjutor.*"*

"*To Thee is the poor man left, Thou wilt be a helper to the orphan.*"

1. Blessed is the poor who has God for his help and support in tribulation; and for his comforter in suffering; who puts all his hope and trust in God, and in his last

* Ps. ix. 36.

hour awaits from Him the crown of glory in the kingdom of eternal bliss.

Voluntary poverty, assumed for the love of Christ, is a precious virtue in the sight of God:—the everlasting recompense is in heaven, under the ward of the angels; thieves cannot steal it, nor the violent bear it away; nor can the murderer make it his prey.

By renouncing all the pleasures and gratifications of the world, the servant of Christ dwells beyond the circle of the dangers and cares which ever surround the rich on earth.

The faithful soul, who for the love of Jesus Christ, and for his kingdom's sake, despoils himself of everything in this world, enjoys true liberty, and possesses all things in Jesus; who for the love of us became poor, and submitted to suffering; who was hung naked on the cross, and had not where to lay his head, nor power to move his hands or feet.

Who amongst us can compare our nakedness or poverty with His?—assuredly no one; wherefore, "His name alone is exalted, the praise of Him is above heaven and earth."*

Oh! salutary poverty, thou now-a-days wouldst meet nothing but contempt among men, unless God had been the first to submit voluntarily to thy privations!

Oh happy poverty,—debarring us from the pride of the eyes, and the occasion of many sins!

2. He is truly poor in spirit, who neither from word nor deed draws forth vanity, and who lest he fall thereby, covets not the honours of the world.

* Ps. cxlviii. 13.

O what an excellent virtue is voluntary poverty, retaining nothing to call its own! It opens to the soul the gates of heaven, it adds new jewels to the crown of glory, that is laid up in heaven; it makes us worthy to receive with the martyrs the palm of patience, after the hardships and sufferings of life, spent in the service of Christ.

For this is truly and faithfully to labour in the service of God, when for His love, we bear with want and all the inconveniences which follow poverty.

Blessed is he who learns how to profit by his wants and infirmities, and who in all the privations he endures, is still submissive to the will of God.

Let not poverty afflict thy heart when thou sufferest want.—If men mock thee, or friends desert thee, give not way to wrath—but turn thy heart to Jesus, who became poor and weak for thy sake. Take comfort in God—in God alone,—if thou wouldst have thy soul rejoice for ever;—for all consolations out of Him, how great soever they seem, are vain, transient, and insufficient.

3. Choose then Jesus Christ for thy only friend and brother: renounce all to follow Him.

Avoid above all the fellowship of those who would turn thee from His holy service; and who by leading thee again into the world, may lead thee to the gates of hell. "For wide is the gate, and broad is the way that leadeth to destruction," saith Jesus Christ, "and many there are, who go in thereat."*

From Him only canst thou find the consolation required; from Him who is able to give the kingdom of heaven to those who for His

* Matt. vii. 13.

sake, renounce the kingdom of this world, and all its vanities; "for the world passes away, and the concupiscence thereof,"* like smoke driven by the wind, and like the flowers of the field that wither away.

Do thou then, my brother, who hast submitted to voluntary poverty, go on courageously in thy holy enterprise; be constant day and night in the service of God, in the peaceful abode thy piety has made choice of. Remember that thou hast spontaneously forsaken thy parents and thy friends, to unite thyself wholly to God; that thou mayest one day find them again, in the kingdom of Christ, and rejoice with them in the company of all the saints.

Thy light afflictions and transitory sorrows here on earth, shall

* 1 John ii. 17.

be recompensed in heaven by the joy of eternal rest.

Reflect often on the sacred wounds of Christ; think of the grievous sores of the poor Lazarus; and it shall profit much during thy last agony, when at the point of death thou art about to pass from time to eternity.

CHAP. XX.
ON THE POOR AND SICK LAZARUS.

"*Ego sum pauper et dolens, Deus adjuva me.*"*

"*I am poor and sorrowful, let thy salvation, O God, set me up.*"

1. This is the prayer of one who is poor and in suffering, whose sighs continually ascend to Heaven.

* Ps. lxviii. 30.

Ye suffering poor, bear patiently, yet a little while, your sorrows and privations, whether of food or raiment; you shall not have long to wait the hour of your deliverance.

Give thanks to God, for it is better to be afflicted now on earth, in company with the poor and the sick, than to be tormented hereafter in hell with the powerful and the wealthy.

Recal to mind thy past transgressions, whether against God or thy neighbour, and bear the chastisement which the Lord sends to afflict thee, in remission of such sins as thou hast not fully repented of, or for which thou hast not made ample satisfaction.

Comfort thy soul by the memory of the cruel sorrows and sacred wounds of Jesus Christ. Thy divine Saviour has endured more bitter stripes for thee, than thou canst suffer for the love of Him.

Comfort thy soul in Him, by recalling to thy memory how Lazarus, poor and covered with sores in this life, was, after death, joyously received into Abraham's bosom; and fear the end of that rich man, who fared sumptuously, but who, after his feasting, was buried in hell, whence there was no departure.

Make now thy choice — thou must either endure for a short while the pains and privations of Lazarus, in his poverty and sickness for the sake of joy eternal in Christ, or partake in the dainties of the rich man in full health, which may end so shortly in sudden death and instant burial in hell to burn in fire for ever with the devil and his angels. Few words are needed by him that is wise.

2. Blessed is he that understands and purifies his heart from all depraved affections, while yet in his power; lest he be condemned to endure the horrible punishments which await the impenitent sinner.

For he on whom holy instructions make no impression, or awaken no sentiment of penance, shall be given over one day to cruel torments, which he shall be constrained to endure fruitlessly and without hope for all eternity.

Lazarus, poor and afflicted in this life, was, after death, delivered from these punishments, and was borne by holy angels in joy and triumph to Abraham's bosom.

Remark also even in the life time of poor Lazarus, the multiplied consolations which the merciful goodness of the Lord offers him in his misery.

We have never heard that he was visited by rich friends to comfort him in his misery;—that he had servants to wait his orders;—that he was surrounded by anxious brethren:—but Jesus tells us, that the dogs came and licked his sores!* these were all that came to him in his misery! no consolations from man, dogs only ministering to him! Can any misery be worse than this? Yet no murmuring or impatient word fell from his lips, but rather thanksgiving and praise:—he that was refused comfort from the instrumentality of man, received it meekly from the sensibility of beasts.

Thou then, weak and suffering brother, murmur not, if, even for a season, thou mayest be deprived of human consolation, or if the goad of thy infirmities press yet more

* Luke xvi. 22.

heavily. Remember that the divine mercy so disposes it, in order that—" Cut and burned in this world, thou mayest not be lost in the next."

Lazarus, perhaps, was not guilty in the sight of God, but of very slight faults; while thou hast often and very grievously offended Him.

Bear then thy infirmities with patience; and if sometimes the consolations of man be withheld, rejoice, nevertheless, that, with Lazarus, thou mayest thereby be worthy to enter the gates of the heavenly kingdom.

CHAP. XXI.

ON THE CLEAR UNDERSTANDING OF THE HOLY SCRIPTURES.

"*Declaratio sermonum tuorum illuminat, et intellectum dat parvulis.*"*

"The declaration of thy words giveth light, and bestoweth understanding on little ones."

1. All that is written in the Old and New Testaments, has been written for our instruction, and with the design of bringing us to serve God faithfully, to inspire in us a horror of what is evil, and a love, boundless, pure, and entire, both in this world, and in that which is to come, for Him who is our sovereign good.

* Ps. cxviii. 130.

Ask humbly for a knowledge of what thou art ignorant of, and ask respectfully from those who are better instructed than thyself, for the right understanding of what thou dost not comprehend. "For the declaration of the words of God giveth light to the hearts of the little ones."

If thou art not capable of rising to the knowledge of the most sublime truths, learn with "the little ones," to know such as are small; it is of such that our Lord Jesus hath said, "Suffer the little children to come to me, for the kingdom of heaven is for such."*

Beware therefore of rashly sounding what is concealed from thy understanding; leave to the Holy Spirit the care of discovering such to thee. Follow His inspirations with a lively faith; for the Holy

* Matt. xix. 14.

Spirit is the source of all truth, and He can never bear testimony to error.

2. If on some points, many persons have doubts, attribute them to the blindness of their spirit, or to their ignorance, and not to the silence or obscurity of the Holy Scriptures, which unfold all the needful documents of eternal salvation.

Read then with pleasure the canonical Scriptures; and to this reading be careful to join the explication of them which the doctors of the Church have given, and thus study to understand them well.

But, nevertheless, let not thy diligence in this study withdraw thee from prayer, or the celebration, or the hearing of the holy mass; for often during holy mass, and in the fervour of prayer, God communicates to devout souls many hidden things which He conceals from those who search curiously, and full of self-sufficiency.

Simple words bring instruction to the little ones and the ignorant; but subtle explanations, which they do not understand, are vain and profitless.

Those that in the refectory, or in the choir, listen attentively to the reading, and seek with prudence to penetrate the mystical sense of the facts recited to them, extract, from all they hear or read, the honey of the word of God.

Whence, though during life, man may ever add something to his knowledge, and discover every day truths of a higher order; yet he shall not attain to the clear and perfect intelligence of the angels; nor shall he enjoy the beatific vision, till, by the help of Christ, he shall have entered into the glory of eternal bliss.

3. Strong and solid food is hurtful to little ones; the weak and babes must be fed with light and delicate nourishment.

Simple music and moderate songs sometimes touch the ear more pleasantly than the swell of voices, which break on the hearing like peals of thunder, and fatigue rather than charm.

Frequent flashes of lightning dazzle the eye; while a moderate light keeps the vision in activity.

The imprudent traveller, who would rashly swim across a deep river, may be drowned; but he that passes by the bridge, reaches the other side without fear of danger.

The lamb passes freely in a narrow path; where the heavy bullock falls, and is caught, but to be led to the slaughter.

So the soul whose faith is simple, and whose submission humble, findeth grace; where the soul full of confidence in itself, loses all it possesses.

High knowledge but too easily puffeth up the proud; and turns, at last, to the confusion of those who glory therein.

4. I have seen simple souls bathed in tears in the fervour of prayer, while those who sang with a loud and melodious voice, felt nothing but dryness of heart. And why this difference?—because the simple and humble soul, in all it says or does, seeks only the glory of God. The voice of the simple in heart, is with God in heaven; the voice of the wandering and dissipated singer, is with men in the streets and public places.

He that attends seriously to the spiritual sense of the Psalms, who reads them slowly, or sings them with attention, tastes, in abundance, the sweetness of devotion. For the Lord is indeed sweet to such as are right in heart, and to those who seek His glory, and not the gratification of their own vanity.

Blessed is the voice of him that sings and declares the praises of God in such a manner, as to fill the hearts of those who hear him with compunction.

5. Before crowing, the cock plumes his wings, as if to prepare himself; so should the good christian or the pious preacher correct his own faults before he undertakes to correct those of others. He that would announce with prudence and success, the word of God, must begin by correcting in himself those vices he condemns in others.

It is thus that St. Paul, while instructing others, humbly calls himself the chief of sinners. " Jesus Christ hath come into this world to save sinners, of whom I am the chief,"* and "who am not worthy to be called an apostle." And why, O most glorious saint?—"because I persecuted the Church of God." How then art thou now become a vessel of election, filled with holiness, and truly worthy of all glory? I owe it not either to myself or to men, but by the vocation and revelation of Jesus Christ, from whom I have learned to be meek and humble of heart, and to be obedient to His gospel. I know of no good in myself; all that I do or teach, I attribute to Him, who, by His grace, hath called me to the faith which I preach, and to which I shall be faithful unto death. For only "by the grace of God I am what I am."† And His grace in me has not been in vain; but remains in me, and shall remain till

* 1 Tim. i. 15. † 1 Cor. xv. 9.

I come to Him who hath redeemed me and saved me by His precious blood.

CHAP. XXII.

ON THE GREAT MERIT OF PATIENCE FOR THE SAKE OF CHRIST.

"*In patientiâ vestra possidebitis animas vestras.*"*

"*In your patience you shall possess your souls.*"

1. When thou art addressed harshly, or reproved unjustly, give not way to the first emotion of anger nor reply sharply; but keep silence, or speak humbly, or suffer with patience like Jesus: for when they brought false witness against

* Luke xxi. 19.

Him, He was silent, and when scourged, He murmured not.

Or if it be necessary or useful to justify thy actions, do it gently and with prudence, and in such a manner as Christ did: when rudely struck by the servant of the high priest, He answered meekly and reasonably; so shalt thou edify others and be freed from confusion.

In every circumstance or contradiction of wicked tongues, be patient, and observe a pious silence towards those who oppose thee.

2. In the spiritual interest of thy soul, never forget how precious a virtue is patience, which adorns the soul with all virtues, and leads to the martyr's glorious palm.

This, Christ hath taught in His words; this, He hath exemplified in His passion;—for when He was accused before the princes of the priesthood, and the ancients of the people, He answered nothing; putting in practice what He before taught, "Learn of me, because I am meek and humble of heart, and you shall find rest to your souls."*

Thou canst not find elsewhere sure peace and true rest, but in God alone, in the practice of sincere humility, and of a mild indulgent patience which overcomes all adversaries.

Put then all thy hope in God, and not in any creature, great or small, for without God all is but vanity; and with God all is good.

* Matt. xi. 29.

CHAP. XXIII.

ON THE GOOD CONVERSATION OF THE HUMBLE CHRISTIAN.

"*Fuge, dilecte mi, fuge.*"*

" Flee away, O my beloved."

1. Why should I flee away? Because of the many dangers which surround thee in the world, and which fall on those who converse therein.

He that would give himself up to the service of God, must love solitude, prayer, study, and labour; and so by useful employments, preserve his soul from the perils of vice, spend his time with fruit, and edify his neighbour.

But he that loves the world, and willingly converses therein, seldom

* Cant. viii. 14.

keeps his heart unspotted, and always returns to his peaceful retreat, with less devotion than when he went out.

Pious and modest conversation is pleasing to all; but harsh and inconsiderate words wound the ears of our friends.

He that loves virtue, speaks the truth, but he that makes use of lying speech, deceives his neighbour, and renders himself odious.

He that is truly humble, seeks not praise for the good he has done; but refers to God all the good that there is in his actions, and attributes to himself only what is evil.

The liar drives Christ from his heart; and he that would fathom the mysteries of religion, confounds himself, and justly falls into error: but he that speaks frankly and straight forward, is honoured and loved by all.

2. We are all brethren, created by the same God; we are all sinners, born of guilty parents; but, by the grace of Christ, we are called to the faith: we are regenerated by the same baptism; and we are all but one body in Christ. Let no one, then, despise or ridicule, or offend his neighbour in any thing:—we ought rather, in conformity to the will of God, to help and instruct him, as far as we are able; doing to him as we would be done by, were we in want.

He that by words of edification, confirms the weak in the faith, feeds the sick with the bread of heaven.

He that consoles the afflicted, gives a cup of life to the thirsty.

He that calms the wrath of his brother by meek words, withholds a dog from biting, by anointing his tongue with honey.

He that checks a wandering tongue, brings much peace to his devout brethren.

He that prefers himself before others, shows but little judgment, and deserves confusion.

He that humbles himself in all things, deserves to receive more abundant grace and honour.

By prayer the pious and humble man breaks the snares of the evil one, and escapes; while the proud, led on by vain glory, falls into his toils, and perishes.

From which may the pious Jesus ever preserve us, and conduct us to the joys of heaven! Amen.

CHAP. XXIV.

ON PRUDENT CONVERSATION, AND BROTHERLY COMPASSION.

" *Medice, cura teipsum.*"*

" *Physician, heal thyself.*"

1. Keep in mind these words, before thou admonish or rebuke thy neighbour; lest haply, in reproving him indiscreetly or unjustly, thou commit a greater fault than his.

The just and prudent man watches his opportunity, and seeks to learn the character and habits of the person to whom he wishes to give advice, lest he drive away or hurt him whom he would correct.

The mouth of the wise and discreet man is worthy of honour, and is like a solid vessel enriched with

* Luke iv. 23.

gold, filled with balm and odoriferous perfumes.

The sanctity of thy words, and the regularity of thy morals, edify those who are attached to the things of this world,—excite the indifferent,—rebuke the negligent,—bring the wandering heart to compunction,—instruct the ignorant, and inflame the fervour of the devout. For the lively example of good men persuades more effectively to contempt of the world, and amendment of life, than the verbose eloquence of worldly learning.

2. It must not be thought, that a desire to instruct and correct others, is a proof of ability or virtue; but to govern oneself well, to receive reproof with pious humility, and to labour fervently in the reform of one's own heart;—this is great wisdom both before God and men.

Learn to put a favourable interpretation on what is doubtful;—never to pass judgment on what is unknown;—to avoid all open evil; to beware of giving scandal;—to bear patiently with the defects or faults of thy brethren;—and to commit to the mercy of God what thou canst not correct.

Reflect that God has borne, and still bears with thee every day in a great many weaknesses; and notwithstanding thou dost not amend them, though thou often declarest thy intention, and that thou hast the will to do so. But His mercy still bears with and awaits thee, to lead thee to penance, and to teach thee thy own infirmities, so that thou mayest humbly sue for pardon, and learn not to despise or rashly condemn thy neighbour.

Be then patient and merciful to thy brother in few things, as God is to thee in many things.

The devout and humble man speaks little, lest his much speaking should be hurtful to internal recollection.

The proud man speaks harshly, and the passionate man disturbs the soul of those he corrects ; as he, himself, is disturbed when corrected. But the meek bears patiently with those he would correct,—makes use of entreaty rather than reproach,— is compassionate for their sins,—and shows himself, indeed, the friend of their souls.

He that seeks to be first, exposes himself to many perils, and becomes despicable.

The lover of vain glory, keeps not long silence, lest he pass for ignorant : he is ashamed of mean and servile employments ; he cannot bear to put himself in the last place, or to sit on the lowest seat. And yet it is the highest honour to practice humility in all things,—to place oneself beneath other men, and voluntarily to fulfil the office of servant to others, for the sake of Christ, who has said, "I am in the midst of you, as he that serveth."*

Learn then, young man, to be silent, if thou wouldst not be covered with confusion, when speaking in the presence of thy elders.

For it is more profitable to be silent, than to speak foolishly.

3. It is a great art to know how to receive correction in silence, and much wisdom to speak modestly and in season; and to say nothing before enlightened men, but what is just and fit.

The fool knows not how to observe either time, or purpose, or order; moreover he often suffers much disquietude from the humiliations his own unadvised dis-

* Luke xxii. 27.

course has justly drawn upon him.

The presumptuous young man, who speaks inconsiderately, is like the fool that stands on a precipice. If he receive advice with docility, correction in silence and commands with submission, there will be great hope that he may make much progress in virtue, and one day flourish like the lily of the valleys.

Great is the pride of him who persists in his own designs, contrary to the will of God, and who refuses submission to the wise counsels of the aged.

Since it is difficult for man in all his words and actions to keep always within the bounds of moderation, and to watch over his soul; hence it is that religious persons love solitude, and seek retreat and silence, to give themselves up to prayer apart from the tumult of the world.

CHAP. XXV.

ON THE UNCERTAIN HOUR OF DEATH, AND THE SPEEDY END OF THIS LIFE.

"*Vigilate, quia nescitis diem neque horam.*"*

"*Watch ye, therefore, because you know not the day nor the hour.*"

1. Blessed is the soul that thinks often of the last hour, when all must be ended in this life;—joys and sorrows, honours and reproaches.

Happy the soul that is as a poor pilgrim travelling towards God;—which despises all the pomp of this world, howsoever great or alluring. For in that last hour all shall perish,—castles, cities, villages, ves-

* Matt. xxv. 13.

sels of gold and silver, all delicate viands, and variegated cups of perfumed wines.

Then shall be mute, lyre, trumpet, pipe and harp.

Then shall be no more sport nor mirth, no more dance nor loud applause, no more songs nor merry laughter, no more the cry of revelry in street or bower, for the hearts of all living shall wither away, and the whole earth shall tremble in the presence of God.

Oh how wise is he who meditates daily on these things, and who prepares, by tears, for the enjoyment of blessings to come, and joy eternal.

2. Blessed is he who separates himself voluntarily from the many snares and perils of this world, and from all that may flatter his sensual appetite.

Blessed is the pilgrim who, in

his exile, weeps, and mourns, and desires to be dissolved, and to be with Christ in the kingdom of heaven.

Blessed is the man who hates this world, and all therein that would allure him to sin; and who flies like Elias, to some monastery in the desert, from the face of numberless dangers, which often drag down the unguarded soul to hell.

Blessed is he that watches day and night against temptation, and who cries out with Elias, "It is enough for me, Lord, take away my soul;"* for it is better for me to die in Thy grace, and when my heart is full of trust in Thee, than to live in this world, surrounded by so many dangers, a witness to evil; for so long as the soul is united to the body, and the body is nourished with the produce of earth, man

* 3 Reg. xix. 4.

cannot be exempt from sin, nor free from temptation, nor assured that he may not hereafter fall.

He then is greatly deceived, and errs like a man foolish of heart, who only desires to live long here below, and to purpose to do many things, when he knows not where he shall be on the morrow.

3. Remember, ye rich and powerful, surrounded with so many enjoyments and delights, what will become of you, when dead and buried in the earth? what will all those riches which you possess, avail you?

Behold! to-day a king, in full enjoyment of life and empire, and to-morrow he is found no more, nor shall his voice again be heard.

To-day, he is seated on a lofty throne, and arrayed in robes of gold, and to-morrow he is laid in the tomb and shall be seen no more.

To-day he is honoured by many, to-morrow he is regarded by none.

To-day he is magnified by all, to-morrow is divested of all his riches and honours, and villas and castles.

To-day he is comely above other men, and numbered with kings; to-morrow he is food for worms, and a stench in the nostrils.

As he came naked into the world, so, like a poor exile, shall he be borne to the grave.

For short is the end of all the pleasures, pomps, and vanities of this world, and death and grief, and mourning and fear, is the lot of all.

His holiness the Pope dies; the Cardinals die; the most powerful sovereigns die; and others succeed, who in their turn soon follow them to the tomb.

No one can be assured of life for a single day, nor obtain from the Pope, nor from all earthly monarchs, the privilege of not dying; nor procure a benefice or an office, from which he can never be ejected.

It often happens that after having obtained favours and places, death comes unexpectedly, and takes all away; so that the supplicant returns from court, as poor and naked as when he first went thither.

4. We read in history of many among the patriarchs and fathers, who lived very long. "Such and such a one lived;" and so of others; but at last it is said of all,—" and he died:" for " we all die, and like waters that return no more, we sink into the earth,"* whence we sprung.

What is the most protracted period of life but a short moment,—a passing wind,—a morning bright-

* 2 Reg. xiv. 14.

ness which fades away,—a traveller who retraces not his steps?

Like a flash of lightning which disappears in the twinkling of an eye, so shall ages disappear; and with them the kingdoms of the earth.

Reckon the hours, the days, the months, and the years of thy life; and tell me whither are they all gone?—they have passed away like a shadow; they have perished like the spider's web,—destroyed by the first wind.

There is nothing lasting, nothing abiding on this earth; of which the body of Adam, and of his sons were all fashioned.

5. Greatness, beauty, pleasures,—all in the world, is full of vanity and frailty.

Then let not these attractions allure, nor their despite or deprivation overwhelm thee.

The fairest colours fade in death,

and the richest ornaments, decked with gold, silver, and precious gems, in the dark tomb are dim and valueless.

Therefore in all thy works, whatever they may be, wherever thou goest, whithersoever thou proceedest, be mindful of the end of life, and of that last hour, which shall come when thou thinkest not.

Blessed is he, who, with the Apostle St. Paul, "desires to be dissolved, and to be with Christ; a thing by far the better"* for us, than to remain a long time in the flesh, on the sea of this world, beaten about by storms, a stranger to God, and ever in fear.

If thou wilt bear Jesus continually in thy heart; if thou wilt love Him sincerely; if every day thou wilt address thy prayers to Him; then mayest thou confidently hope

* Phil. i. 23.

to one day enter into His kingdom; for He hath said, "where I am, there also shall my minister be."*

Blessed is the servant, who, at his last hour, shall deserve to hear those sweet words of Jesus Christ, " Well done, good and faithful servant, because thou hast been faithful over a few things, I will place thee over many things; enter thou into the joy of thy Lord."

* John xii. 26. † Matt xxv. 21.

CHAP. XXVI.

OF THE ETERNAL PRAISE OF GOD, AND THE DESIRE OF ETERNAL GLORY.

" *Lauda, anima mea, Dominum.*"*

"*Praise the Lord, O my soul,*" *-from whom cometh all good, both now and forever more.*

1. Thus oughtest thou to refer all to Him, as to the first beginning and last end of all good. Thou oughtest to praise Him with sentiments of inmost gratitude, in order that the gift of His heavenly grace may flow upon thee anew in larger streams, and with continued increase; until thou wilt have arrived at the fountain of life eternal, to the country of eternal charity,

* Ps. cxlv. 2.

and to the beatific vision of His divine presence and glory.

For thee there is nothing better or more salutary, more sweet or agreeable, more worthy, more exalted, more happy, more perfect, more blessed, than to love God most ardently, and to praise Him without measure. This, I would tell thee a hundred times;—this I would repeat a thousand times. There is no study so elegant, no employment so noble, as that of loving and praising God, thy Creator and Redeemer, with all thy heart, with all thy soul, and with all thy strength.

Do this as long as thou hast life, and being, and intellect; let this be the only object of all thy discourse, and of all thy actions, night and day, at morning, at midday, at evening, at every hour, and every instant.

2. Unite thyself to Him as strictly as thy strength and knowledge permit, wholly and entirely;—in order that to thee, God may be all things, and that, before all and above all. He may be loved, blessed, praised, and exalted by thee for all ages, and that thou mayest enjoy together with Him a happiness without end.

Exult, then, O faithful soul, in the Lord thy God, as the blessed Virgin Mary rejoiced in Jesus Christ her Saviour.

Exult and praise thy God, who has made and redeemed thee, for to God thou art indebted for all those many and inestimable benefits which thou dost daily receive from His merciful bounty; for even wert thou a holy angel, thy gratitude as such would still be inadequate to His goodness and infinite grandeur.

Praise Him nevertheless, thank Him, as a mortal man dependant on His mercy, and ever seeking and imploring it with tearful perseverance.

Cease not to pray to Him and to praise Him, and although thou shouldst often unhappily fall into sin, and thereby offend Him, despair not, but rather humble thyself, and pray with more fervour.

Love, and thou shalt be loved: love purifies the soul from all past faults; cleanses and cures all its wounds—enlightens the spirit—inflames the heart—drives away sadness, and begets inward joy; such as the world knoweth not, and flesh and blood can never feel.

Praise God, and thou shalt be praised; bless Him, and thou shalt be blessed; sanctify His name, and thou shalt be made holy; magnify Him and thou shalt be made great;

glorify Him, and thou shalt be glorified by Him in soul as well as in body.

3. *The Soul.*—But when shall these things be? When wilt thou open my mouth, to sing Thy praises for ever? when will my heart and my soul rejoice together with Thy saints in glory?

The Lord.—Wait yet a little while, and when the trumpet shall sound, thou shalt see great wonders: then shall I give to my saints, in recompense of their pains, and labours, rest and life eternal,—what wishest thou more?

The Soul.—Absolutely nothing, O Lord; Thou alone art sufficient for me, my God; Thou who givest life eternal, to those who love and praise Thee; Thou who renderest goods, vast, inestimable, and eternal, for what is valueless and perishable.

The Lord.—Give then thyself to God, and all that thou hast; give Him all thy actions, all thy knowledge, all thy faculties; and thou shalt be richer, and dearer to Him than thou hast ever yet been.

Say with St. Paul, that " we are as having nothing, and possessing all things " in God;* poor, afflicted, despised, in the eyes of men, but rich and " always rejoicing "† in the Lord, and sure of receiving our reward in heaven.‡

4. *The Soul.*—O Lord God, my salvation, and my God! when shall my soul enjoy in Thy kingdom the gracious light of Thy countenance? Oh! when wilt thou enlighten all the darkness of my spirit in the splendour of eternal light?

When wilt thou remove from my heart every obstacle which prevents me from uniting myself inti-

* 2 Cor. vi 10.   † 1 Thes. v. 16.   ‡ 2 Tim. iv. 8.

mately to Thee. O true peace, supreme blessedness, perfect felicity!

O Lord, when shall I be able to follow Thee, free from all hindrance and restraint; and go wherever Thou shalt lead the way?

When shall I be able with mine eyes to see Thee clearly, without a glass, without a riddle, without a parable, without a figure, without uncertainty, without the doubts, and discussions, and questions of the learned?

When shall it be given me to fully understand all these things which the Holy Scriptures present to my belief,—all these things which I have read in various authors;—all these things which in various places I have heard from learned instructors concerning my God, concerning the Angels, their different choirs, concerning the glory and beatitude of the heavenly country, concerning the peace and joy ineffable of the celestial inhabitants!

When shall I be there? when shall I be able to appear in Thy blessed presence; to contemplate Thy radiant countenance, and the glory of Thy heavenly kingdom, with the cherubim and seraphim, and all the saints?

But the hour is not yet come; the gates of heaven are yet closed to me; wherefore, O my God, my heart is afflicted; and my mouth uttereth groanings, as long as I tarry here, and until I come to Thee, my God.

CHAP. XXVII.

OF THE PRAISES SUNG BY THE HOLY ANGELS IN HEAVEN.

"*In conspectu angelorum psallam tibi.*"*

"*I will sing to thee in the sight of the angels.*"

1. O King most High! O Lord supreme! O God worthy of all praise! Creator of all things, of Angels and of men! how long shall I tarry sojourning on earth, far removed from thee and all thy holy angels in heaven? Poor and wretched creature as I am, how long shall I eat with men the bread of toil and of sorrow? How long shall I be deprived of the bread of angels,—that food so ex-

* Ps. cxxxvii. 1.

quisite, containing " all that is delicious and the sweetness of every taste.*"

2. O Lord, when shall I hear the sound of Thy praises sung by Thy holy angels in heaven; as the blessed apostle John when in exile, heard the voices of many angels singing together,—" Holy, Holy, Holy?"†

Oh that I were one of that holy company, and had a voice like unto theirs! Oh how willingly would I praise Thee in company with them; beyond the loudest Canticles in heaven would I sing thy praise and magnify Thy holy name to all eternity!

Oh ye Cherubim and Seraphim, how sweetly, how beautifully, how fervently, how excellently ye sing those joyous hymns in presence of your God, without lassitude, with-

* Wisdom xvi. 20. † Apoc. iv 8.

out fatigue, without cessation in eternal felicity!

3. To me, therefore, all human accent appears harsh; every song, unharmonious; every psalm spiritless and dry; every music disagreeable; every instrument out of tune; every joy appears extreme sadness; every laughter, mourning; every kind of meat and drink, insipid and tasteless; all flesh, so much grass; all wine, gall and vinegar; all honey, poison; every thing pleasant, disagreeable; all beauty, an object of disgust; every ornament, so much deformity; all honour and glory, smoke and vanity; everything precious and valuable, contemptible and disgusting;—in one word, all things appear as nothing in comparison with life eternal, glory without end, and never ceasing joy in the presence of God and His angels; who

day and night for ever sing in highest note, the praises of the holy and the glorious Trinity.

4. Since then I am unable to soar aloft to these sublime and heavenly canticles, or fully to comprehend them, I bewail my sad fate, and despise myself before God and men, —bending my knees and humbly asking pardon :—for in truth all my works are nothing, O Lord, without Thy grace and Thy mercy, which in so great bounty, Thou dost display in all Thy creatures without limit of number or measure. " O the depth of the riches of the wisdom and of the knowledge of God !"* how profound and how just are Thy judgments from age to age, upon the good and the bad, —the grateful and the ungrateful, —upon the pious and the impious : so that no one can fathom Thy

* Rom. xi. 33.

words; no one can with justice, complain of events that happen unexpectedly in the course of human affairs. Wherefore be Thou ever blessed, O my God!

CHAP. XXVIII.

A PRAYER OF THE DEVOUT LOVER OF GOD.

"*Dirigatur, Domine, oratio mea, sicut incensum in conspectu tuo.*"*

"*Let my prayer be directed as incense in thy sight.*"

1. I desire, O Lord my God, in every place and at all times, to join Thy saints, and all Thy creatures, in devoutly praising and blessing Thee;—in publishing Thine infi-

* Ps. cxl. 2.

nite perfections;—in loving Thee perfectly;— in glorifying Thee without ceasing, and in exalting the greatness and glory of Thy holy name for ever; for Thou, O Lord, Thou art my God, and I am Thy poor servant.

For thou art my light and my hope, O my God! Thou art my strength and my patience, my praise and my glory, O my God!

Thou art my wisdom, my prudence, my beauty, and all my sweetness, O my God!

Thou art my music and harp, my organ and timbrel, O my God!

Thou art the psalm that brings gladness to my heart, my hymn, my canticle, and my song of joy, O my God!

Thou art my casque and breastplate, my bow and my sword, O my God!

2. Thou art my treasure, my

gold and silver; and the talent with which I am to pay all my debts, O my God!

Thou art my dwelling-place, my fortress, and my palace, O my God!

Thou art my shield and banner, my tower of strength, and the defence of my life, O my God!

Thou art my garden and orchard, my bower of green, and cool retreat, O my God!

Thou art my refectory and table, my meat and my drink, O my God! for all food not prepared and seasoned by thee, seems to me stale and flat, O my God!

Thou art my aromatical plant, and balsam of sweetness, my spikenard and choice myrrh, and most precious ointment, O my God!

Thou art my rose and lily, my wreath and garland, O my God!

Thou art my dormitory, and my

bed, my napkin and covering art thou, O my God!

3. Thou art my light and my lamp,—my lustre and star that enlightens me, O my God!

Thou art my book written within and without; my Bible, in which all the Holy Scripture is contained, and the teacher who gives to me understanding, O my God!

Thou art my kind instructor, and skilful physician, kindly administering the remedies requisite for my spiritual welfare, O my God!

For in Thee I find all things, and all that I have is through Thy mercy and goodness; and I feel that all that I seek, or all that I desire out of Thee, is of little or no profit to my soul.

Open then my heart to Thy holy law; "restore unto me the joy of

Thy salvation;"* enlarge my heart that I may run in Thy ways; confirm me by Thy words, for Thou alone canst help me, and lead me to eternal life.

O Lord, my God, hear the vows I address to Thee, in joy, in tribulation, in health, or sickness,—in all things,—I commend me into Thy hands, and desire to bless Thee for ever and ever. Amen.

* Ps. l. 14.

CHAP. XXIX.

ON UNION OF THE HEART WITH GOD.

"*Convertere anima mea in requiem tuam, quia Dominus benefecit tibi.*"*

"*Turn, O my soul, into thy rest, for the Lord hath been bountiful to thee.*"

1. For verily He is thy rest, and thy peace, thy life, thy salvation, and thy happiness: all, therefore, that thou dost, all that thou seest, all that thou hearest of good, refer to the glory of God, that so thou mayest have peace and a good conscience.

Put not thy trust,—rejoice not,—in thyself or others, but cling to

* Ps. cxiv. 7.

God alone, purely, steadily, entirely: dwell with Him who giveth and worketh all in all, by the might of His goodness, and the greatness of His mercy.

Oh, who will give me grace to refer all to the praise and honour of God?—with all my strength to do all the good that I am bound, or am able to do;—to be so insensible to the vanities of earth, that none of them, whether great or small, shall be able to draw me from Him;—to turn me away from his service;—to overcast my soul with trouble, or in anywise to hinder me?

But, perhaps, it is not possible for me to obtain such a state in this life? Oh, say not so, for all is possible to God, and He can, instantly, by the sweet cords of His love, unite the devout soul to Himself: for this pure and perfect love of God, can so act in a moment, whensoever it pleases Him, that forgetful of all creatures, the soul may be wholly united to Him alone, and vehemently enflamed, yea melted, by the fire of his love.

2. Oh, my God and my love, when, in this place of exile, shall I be wholly united to Thee? when shall I love Thee with all the strength of my soul—that strength which Thou alone hast given and graciously infused?

May all created beings keep silence before Thee, O my God! Speak Thou only to my soul, O God, blessed eternally! assist it, help it, enlighten it, Thou that art all in all, and whose brightness is above the stars of the firmament!

Happy is the soul, which, being afflicted in this world, is comforted of God;—which being unknown to men,—is known to the holy angels; —neglected by the wicked, but sought after by the good;—despised by the proud, but loved by the humble;—separated from the children of the world, but united to the servants of God;—scorned by the great, but honoured by the little ones;—dead to the world, but alive unto God;—afflicted in the flesh, but rejoicing in spirit;—weak in health, but strong in mind;—downcast in countenance, but upright in conscience;—burthened by toil, but strengthened in prayer;—bent under the weight of infirmities, but raised up again by interior consolations, and prisoned in this world by the bonds of the flesh, but in spirit rapt to heaven, and joined with Christ.

3. Blessed is he who has Jesus and Mary, the angels and saints of God for his friends in this life;—for guides on his way;—for advisers in doubt;—for masters in his

studies ;—for readers at his table ; —for companions in his solitude ;—for familiars in his conversation ;—for fellow-singers in choir ;—for guards in danger ;—for help in trials ;—for defenders against his enemies ;—for intercessors after sin ;—for assistants in his last hour ;—for comforters in his agony ;—for advocates in the day of judgment ;—for patrons before God ;—and for joyous congratulators, introducing him to the courts of heaven !

O religious and devout soul, who hast forsaken the world, thy family, and home, receive now God for thy father ;—Jesus for thy brother ; —Mary for thy mother ;—the angels for thy friends ;—and thy fellow-religious for thy relations.

Look on all the faithful as thy neighbours ;—the old men as thy uncles ;—the young men as thy brothers;—the married women as thy mothers;—the young maidens as thy sisters;—the poor as thy friends;—the travellers as thy cousins;—the meek and humble of heart as thy companions;—the sober and chaste as thy mess-mates;—the sick and afflicted as thy familiars;—the distressed and despised and scorned as the dear friends of thy heart;—the pious as those most worthy of honour;—and all those who despise the world, and serve Christ, as co-heirs in the kingdom of Heaven.

This is the holy generation and noble offspring born of God, pleasing to God, founded on faith, strengthened by hope, adorned by charity, armed with patience, proved by the fire of tribulation, and ever firm in constancy.

CHAP. XXX.

ON TRUE PEACE, TO BE SOUGHT FOR IN GOD ALONE.

"*Pax vobis! Ego sum, nolite timere.*"*

"*Peace be to you. It is I, be not afraid.*"

1. Christ Jesus is the foundation of our safety, and the only source of true peace.

He that loves Christ, enjoys peace and rest in him—desires nothing out of him, nothing more than him.

The peace of the faithful soul here below consists in suffering for the love of God and in the name of Christ; and whoso thinketh otherwise, is in error, and deceiveth him-

* Jo. vi. 20.

self. Vain is the labour of him who placeth not God at the beginning of all his thoughts, of all his actions:—who seeks not,—desires not God alone. "There is no peace to the wicked, saith the Lord God,"* but those who love thy law, O Lord, shall enjoy abundantly the sweetness of thy peace.

2. The peace which Christ taught and promised, is to be found in profound humility,—in a complete denial of our own will,—in the mortification of our depraved inclinations,—in the contempt of worldly praise, and of all consolation in perishable and passing things.

Watch then over thy heart within, lest thou be seduced by its attractive deceit; and watch over thy senses without, lest thou seek

* Isaiah lvii. 21.

for gratifications injurious to thy soul.

And yet created things often serve to our spiritual advancement, when we refer the use made of them directly and entirely to the honour and glory of God:—or when used with moderation and discretion for our own pressing necessities, or for the good of our brethren.

3. But their beauty often becomes to us an occasion of sin, when beheld with looks full of curiosity—of concupiscence—of passion:—for then they produce in our souls desires and affections contrary to the purpose and glory of God. Thus the unwary are often overcome by evil, and fall, where the wise and good are watchful to preserve their virtue.

Remember that riches tempt, money corrupts, and pleasure stains the soul; that much feasting chokes it; knowledge puffeth up; power breeds self sufficiency, and honours beget pride.

Perverse souls are disgusted with humility; and vain, empty praise seduces the light and unstable.

There is not only absolute folly but downright frenzy in loving and seeking after pleasure, which cannot satisfy the soul nor give the heart repose; for all that is of the world shall fail, and is of short duration: nothing but God is perfect, and nothing but Him should we regard as sovereign beatitude and highest good.

4. Beware then, lest beauty of form, nobility of birth, or height of office, engross thy affections and occupy thy mind, if thou wouldst not be deceived and lose the peace of thy heart, and the purity of thy

soul. All things are vain, slippery, and hurtful, at least, if not referred to God, from whom cometh all good, and in whom all things live and move, and have their being.

Glory not then, O frail and mortal man, who in so many things art guilty, so prone to fall into sin, —so weak withal, and unable to stand in virtue; trust not thyself overmuch, nor be too confident in thyself or others, by high thoughts and vain presumption, but offer and ascribe to God, without restriction or reserve, all the good thou perceivest, whether in thyself or others, or in any other created thing.

Then wilt thou find in Christ that peace of heart, and sweet repose, which may be vainly sought in all created things : then will be accomplished in thee and of thee, the sweet and holy promise of

Christ on the mount, " Blessed are the clean of heart, for they shall see God :"*—to Whom be praise, honour, and glory, from every creature, now and for ages of ages. Amen.

CHAP. XXXI.

THAT OUR INTENTION SHOULD BE PURE AND ALWAYS DIRECTED TOWARDS GOD.

" *Oculi mei semper ad Dominum, quoniam ipse evellet de laqueo pedes meos.*"†

"*My eyes are ever towards the Lord; for he shall pluck my feet out of the snare.*"

1. In all thy thoughts, words, and actions, have always a right

* Matt. v. 8.   † Ps. xxiv. 15.

and pure intention towards God; that so thou mayest do all things to His praise, honour and glory, and to the edification of thy neighbour. For God is the source of all good, and the great giver of eternal rewards; and if thou wouldst not lose the fruit of thy labours, He alone ought to be the beginning and sole end of all thy good works: and if thou wert fully penetrated with the terror of God's righteous judgments, vanity would never take possession of thy heart.

2. Vain glory and a desire of being praised in public by all, is a most deadly poison. It is most excessive vanity, and certain indication of pride, and directly opposed to the grace of God.

What then wilt thou do? or in whom wilt thou place thy hope and confidence? Not surely in thyself, nor in man, nor in earthly creatures; nor in the stars of heaven; but in God alone, thy Creator, who made and sustains thee, as well as all created things, by the might of His right hand, and He needs none as help or support. Call out then, with the holy king David, " My eyes are ever towards the Lord; for He shall pluck my feet out of the snare:"* adding these words, " Lord, all my desire is before thee, and my groaning is not hidden from thee."†

3. Renouncing then the deceitful consolations and counsels of men, fly in thy need unto thy God; place all thy trust in Him; call upon Him with fervent prayer and holy desires, for "He will pluck thy feet out of the snare, so that thou mayst be not moved out of the way" of virtue and true hu-

* Ps. xxiv. 15.   † Ps. xxxvii. 10.

mility, but persevere steadfastly in the service of God unto the end.

Every good work done for the sake of God, maketh the conscience glad, brings light to the mind, and meriteth a greater increase of grace ; but every bad action brings sorrow to him that commits it, stains his good name, and obstructs the influence of divine consolation.

He that doth anything through motives of vain glory, puts out his light with the wind of ostentation ; and he, who is virtuous that he may please men, and stand high in their esteem, shall quickly be overthrown by an angry God, and grovel in the mire.

Rejoice not then, like fools, in the smiles of the world, but rather let the sense of thy own frailty keep thee in the fear of God. Thy frequent falls and constant tendency to error, should teach thee to entertain an humble and mean opinion of thyself.

4. Beware of giving too much praise to any man in this life, for thou knowest not what he may become hereafter: neither rashly condemn him that falleth; for touched by his tears, God may shortly grant him grace to rise again. Pray for all men, and commend all unto God.

Be vile in thine own eyes, so shalt thou be great in the sight of God, who hath respect to the humble, but knowing the proud afar off, He will suddenly cast him down.

If thou art despised by men, and if others are preferred before thee, be not cast down into the excess of sadness; it is better and safer, doubtless, to be humbled by men, in company with the meek and simple, than to be cast off by God with the rich and the lofty-minded.

Shun the praises of men; fear to be exalted; blush at proffered honours; fly from human respect; strive rather to live secluded. Prefer, before all, the service due to God, the study of holy books, and perseverance in prayer.

That man is not without praise and honour, who, for the sake of God, despiseth praise and honour; nor is he without consolation, who holdeth all the joys of this world as nothing, and who gladly endureth every thing contrary to his inclination, for the love of Christ, and whose daily aspirations and sighs are to be united to Him in heaven.

CHAP. XXXII.

THE PRAYER OF AN HUMBLE AND A CONTRITE SPIRIT.

"*Ad te, Domine, levavi animam meam,*"* "*qui habitas in cœlis.*"†

"To thee have I lifted up my soul, O Lord," "who dwellest in heaven."

1. O Lord God! whose wisdom and justice regulate all things in heaven and in earth,—angels, men, and every created being, instead of the exalted praise and thanksgiving which are Thy due, vouchsafe to accept in offering, the tribulations and anguish of a heart truly sorry for its manifold transgressions. Whatever is of evil in me, do Thou turn into good; and the good, do

* Ps. xxiv. 1.   † Ps. cxxii 1.

Thou still convert into better; for the glory of Thy name, and the eternal salvation of my soul. Thou knowest all my infirmity, all my ignorance, and the wonted fickleness of my mind and memory:—how quickly I wander hither and thither; very often alas! still farther from Thee. Spare me, O Lord, according to the multitude of Thy mercies, and direct my wandering footsteps to Thee. Preserve my heart in Thy presence, day and night ever engaged,—as far as this frail body will bear,—in devout prayer and holy meditation.

2. I desire, O Lord, to appease Thy benign countenance with sacred offerings and prayers. particularly with the needy man's three mites, viz.:—contrition of heart, confession of mouth, and humble satisfaction. O Lord, my God, supremely loved, be mindful of me

Thy poor servant, since I am a weak mortal, not a pure angel; a vile sinner, not an innocent lamb; tepid in prayer, not fervent in contemplation:—Therefore unworthy to be counted Thy servant, nor regarded among Thy pious worshippers. O Lord God of my heart, deign then to accept the prayer of Thy humble servant; accept my bitter sorrow for past offences, as Thou receivest the sweet songs, and harmonious jubilations of all the celestial inhabitants. Although I often fall, and my soul is sad from my wretched frailty, still do I not, nor shall I ever, despair of Thy mercy and pardon.

Through the whole period of my life, I cease not, nor shall I ever cease, to sing Thy praise, but I shall ever honour and magnify Thy name, until my soul will go to seek Thee, my God; for to praise and love Thee above all things without cessation, is the supreme happiness of the angels and saints in Thy heavenly kingdom.

CHAP. XXXIII.

OF HOLY FELLOWSHIP WITH JESUS AND WITH HIS SAINTS.

*"Quæsite Deum, et vivet anima vestra."**

"Seek ye after God, and your soul shall live."

1. There is nothing better,—nothing more beneficial to the soul than to seek after God alone. He that seeketh any other thing, shall end by finding nothing.

If, therefore, thou wouldst have

* Ps. lxviii. 33.

a friend to give true consolation in affliction, go to Jesus;—approach His crib with the shepherds,* come with the Magi, to adore Him in the arms of his mother;† follow Him to the temple with Simeon and Anna;‡ to the city with Martha;§ to the sepulchre, with Mary Magdalen:‖ or filled with sentiments of the most sweet and lively joy, join the apostles in the upper chamber, to receive with them the Holy Spirit.**

Blessed is he, that in these and other holy places, devoutly seeks Jesus, not in body only, but in spirit and in truth.

Blessed is he who, at all times, and in every place, seeketh Jesus from the bottom of his heart, and who burns with an ardent desire to enjoy His presence, and to pre-

---
* Luke i.   † Matt. ii.   ‡ Luke ii.
§ Luke x.   ‖ Jo. xx.   ** Acts ii.

pare himself every day for the bright vision, and presence of Christ.

Blessed is he who, in his life, follows Jesus to Calvary, and bears his cross with Him; for his divine Saviour shall assist him in his last hour, and he shall not fear the sentence of reprobation destined for the wicked.

2. Seek not only Jesus, but the disciples of Jesus, and all that love Jesus; and all, who for His love, bear patiently the pains and sorrows of this life: for the love of Jesus and His friends maketh a man despise the world, and driveth away all that is impure or vain.

Renounce then those friends, those acquaintances, those companions, who would offer an obstruction in thy retreat or devotion; and for thy singular consolation, seek in secret retirement to entertain thyself with the holy apostles, and brethren of Jesus, that they may speak to thee of the kingdom of God, and declare how great is the happiness of the elect; and how, by passing through many tribulations, thou mayest attain their happy society.

Come then, before all holy saints, men or women, citizens of the heavenly court, withdraw thyself from the tumult of the world : retire into the secret tabernacle and oratory of the blessed Virgin Mary, and seek there by constant prayer, for all necessary consolation.

3. Listen to the angel of the Lord, announcing to Mary the incarnation of Christ, and the redemption of the human race.

O blessed day and happy hour! if thou canst rest there in company with the angel Gabriel, and the blessed Virgin Mary, and learn from their mouths the mysteries of heaven; believing, most firmly, in the truth of all things which were declared by the angel to Mary, even as she believed God, and His angel sent from heaven.

Then turn to the desert, and seek diligently John the Baptist, the precursor of our Lord Jesus Christ, where he lies hid; and on bended knees humbly say with much devotion:—

"Hail, John, the most holy and beloved friend of Jesus Christ, I have often heard of thy many virtues, and the wonders of thy admirable life; I have heard of the miraculous sanctity of thy birth; I have heard with what religious austerity thou livedst in the desert from thine infancy, that so thou mightest preserve thy spotless purity in word and thought."

4. Ask of him how long he remained alone in the desert, and

dwell with him there as long as thou canst, or time will allow.

Learn of him what was his meat or his drink, and who ministered to his wants; see if his father or mother sent any thing to him; or whether they came to him, or he to them: or whether the angel Gabriel descended on him to reveal to him many hidden things, or even whether Jesus appeared in person to him, and strengthened his hand, as it is written in the gospel: "For the hand of the Lord was with him."*

Whatsoever revelations St. John the Baptist had been favoured with in the desert, do thou commit thyself entirely to the Holy Spirit, with whom he was filled, by whom he was instructed,—who formed him, and adorned his life with all virtues;—who, in the desert, in the

* Luke i. 66.

world, in prison, and in chains, watched over him, and received his soul at last, as it bore away the glorious palm of martyrdom.

5. Approach then to the apostles of Christ; seek out St. Peter, and follow him to the temple to pray, or ascend with him into the upper chamber, "to receive the Holy Spirit."*

Follow St. Paul to Damascus, to Ephesus, and go with him through all dangers, to preach the gospel of Christ, not in body, but in spirit.

Behold how his labours exceed all; how often he prays, and how frequently in his prayers and meditations, he is rapt up into heaven.

It is true these great favours are not vouchsafed to all; and yet the apostle, humbling himself to the lowest, says, "I do not count myself to have apprehended:"† and

* Acts. ii. † Phil. iii. 13.

elsewhere, when teaching the humble, that they ought to conform themselves to the life and passion of Jesus Christ, he says, " I judged not myself to know any thing among you, but Jesus Christ and Him crucified."*

Follow, then, St. Paul, for he will lead thee by the straight path unto Christ, and by the way of the cross to heaven.

6. Go then further, and in the parts of Achaia, listen to the apostle Andrew, preaching the faith of Christ; hear his words from the cross on which he was nailed, for the name of Jesus Christ; engrave them on thy heart, and study to fulfil with joy, through the inspiration and assistance of the Holy Spirit, all that he declares of the passion of Christ, and the praises of the holy cross.

* 1 Cor. ii. 2.

Seek then St. James the Greater, who suffered martyrdom under Herod; drink, with him, of the chalice of sorrow in this miserable life;—bearing patiently with all suffering, for the love of God, and the salvation of thy soul.

7. Next proceed, and seek John, the beloved apostle of Christ, who, for the name of Jesus, was sent into exile; and separated from the world, and all its cares and concerns; where, enlightened by divine revelation, he wrote in symbolic and mysterious style in the Apocalypse, the state of the church militant and triumphant; and after this, he wrote his gospel, to instruct and console all churches, and all the faithful therein, and give testimony, last of all, to the divinity of Jesus Christ.

Read and study well these, and the other books of Holy Scripture, as much as thy understanding will allow, and thy wants require in this thy exile, here on earth: not with a view to pass for wise and learned, in the eyes of men, but that thou mayest become meek and patient, humble and obedient even unto death.

8. Go also, and for thy consolation seek the other apostles, employed in the service of God, enduring martyrdom for the faith and love of Christ, and leading the faithful to virtue, both by their example, and by their words.

Behold St. James, the brother of our Lord, writing his canonical Epistle, wherein is contained the rule of a Christian life, and the whole perfection of our religion.

Seek St. Thomas in the Indies; that apostle who reverently touched the wounds of Christ, and who, believing firmly, cried out with an ardent love, " My Lord and my God."*

With a like holy zeal, seek the holy apostle and learned evangelist Matthew, writing, in the Hebrew character, the gospel of Christ, for the instruction of all the world, and for the salvation of all people, and nations and tongues.

With an equal ardour and affection, follow the other holy apostles and disciples of Jesus Christ; each one, in the several relations and places, preserving the word of life, teaching the people, and labouring unto death in the vineyard of the Lord.

Behold these are the saints and friends of God, who, at the price of their blood, and by the crown of martyrdom, merited eternal life. Read with pleasure the recital of their labours and sufferings, and

* John. xx. 28.

thou wilt be consoled in thy labours, and light affliction; for whatever thou mayest do or suffer, it is as nothing in comparison with that which the martyrs and all the blessed have done and suffered for Christ in the service of God.

CHAP. XXXIV.

ON PLACING OUR SOVEREIGN GOOD AND FARTHEST AIM IN GOD ALONE.

"*Satiabor cum apparuerit gloria tua.*"*

"*I shall be satisfied when thy glory shall appear.*"

1. *The Soul.*—O Lord, how shall man attain to this glory?

* Ps. xvi. 15.

Jesus Christ.—By the contempt of himself, and all earthly things, and by an ardent love of all heavenly things.

The saints who rejoice in heaven, and all the faithful who still combat here below, against the allurements of sin,—are my witnesses for this.

But those who are far from attaining the eternal glory and sovereign beatitude, are the proud angels of darkness, the infidel Pagans, the perverse Jews, hardened heretics, and carnal men, who seduced by the pleasures of the world, and neglecting the service of God, propose no other end in all their actions, than the enjoyment of earthly goods, the honour and esteem of men.

Ah! woe is me, O God;—such infatuated persons are driven about in every sense, in painful journeys, in severe study, in constant watchings, solicitous without ceasing, and labouring without relaxation, to increase and preserve those enjoyments which make them slaves to their desires: and when they have received a part of what they thirst for, when they have obtained directly or indirectly the object of their labours, still are they not satisfied; they wish to rise still higher, for their vanity will leave nothing below them; they puff themselves up, and think themselves wise and worthy of the esteem of man, and the homage of their brethren. Howbeit in all this, what is there but vanity, frailty, and nothing; whatsoever they desire, whatever they seek, is lost as regards the great work of their salvation, and full of danger to the welfare of their souls.

2. In very deed ye are in error

and deceive yourselves, ye who in the world find sweetness, ye for whom this present world is full of pleasantness; for none of these enjoyments are secure, and every day ye draw nearer to death, and to the judgment of God.

For there is nothing in this world so agreeable but what has annexed to it somewhat of bitterness; whatsoever of loveliest, best and sweetest, created things can offer you—all are insufficient to satisfy the soul; they cannot deliver it from evil; they cannot fill it with good, nor keep it in endless joy; God alone, who is eternal, immense, and sovereignly good, God alone can produce in us these blessed effects. He is the creator of all things, visible and invisible, of angels and men,—before all—above all—and in all—God blessed for ever.

3. Can the blessed spirits in Heaven, or those on earth, think or speak worthily of Him? Ah no! for He is above all that a created being can conceive, and in His sight all things are vain and valueless. Miserably deceived is the unhappy soul, that, apart from God, seeks and fosters those affections, which would turn it away from the love and honour of God, but which will leave it at the end in poverty and abject indigence.

A PRAYER.

4. *O Lord, great and wonderful are thy works! and to fathom or understand any one of them, is not possible for me or any living creature. What therefore shall I do, whereas I am unable either to comprehend things so far above my capacity, penetrate the secrets of*

heaven, or contemplate in company with angels, the face of my God? I confess myself unworthy to enjoy happiness so great, and converse with the saints in heaven. Therefore will I humble and despise myself, before God and man, as long as I live, and I will be as nothing in my own eyes; that God may have pity on me a miserable sinner, now, and all days of my life.

In the bitterness of my soul, I shall think over my past years, in which I have provoked His wrath and indignation, and with groans and weeping I will appease my God, whom I have so often offended by words, by deeds, by seeing, by hearing, and by the other senses: which had been given me to serve my Creator, with all my heart, all the days of my sojourn here below.

But lest I should become dejected and fall into despair on account of *my numerous transgressions, I will call to mind, O Lord, the multitude of Thy mercies which are from eternity; until by Thy divine grace and favour, I may be enabled to reach Thee in safety. Deliver me, O Lord, from all those dangers and calamities which so often assail me unprepared, and frequently distract my mind from the contemplation of Thy heavenly goods. Assist me, O God infinitely good, and place me nigh unto Thee: lest I should begin to wander far from my Supreme Good, which Thou art, O my God! For in Thee alone is all my good. Give me Thyself, and it sufficeth my soul, O Lord, thou God of my salvation. Amen.*

THE END

OF

THE VALLEY OF LILIES.

www.ingramcontent.com/pod-product-compliance
Lightning Source LLC
Chambersburg PA
CBHW030805230426
43667CB00008B/1078